The View from East Jerusalem

The View from East Jerusalem

JOHN A. LAPP

Introduction by
Frank H. Epp

HERALD PRESS
Scottdale, Pennsylvania
Kitchener, Ontario
1980

Library of Congress Cataloging in Publication Data

Lapp, John Allen.
  The view from East Jerusalem.

  1. Jewish-Arab relations—1973-   —Addresses,
essays, lectures. 2. Near East—Politics and government—1945-   —Addresses, essays, lectures. I. Title
DS119.7.L29   327.5694'017'4927   79-26122
ISBN 0-8361-1920-7

THE VIEW FROM EAST JERUSALEM
Copyright © 1980 by Herald Press, Scottdale, Pa. 15683
    Published simultaneously in Canada by Herald Press,
    Kitchener, Ont. N2G 4M5
Library of Congress Catalog Card Number: 79-26122
International Standard Book Number: 0-8361-1920-7
Printed in the United States of America
Design: Alice B. Shetler

15 14 13 12 11 10 9 8 7 6 5 4 3 2 1

To the
extraordinary Jerusalem Staff of
Mennonite Central Committee

Yacoub 'Amer
Bishara Awad
Salwa Awad
Mariam Barakat
Mohammed Dajani
Sahir Dajani
Jon Ebersole
Adla Issa
Adele Khoury
William Knopp
Odette Abu Leil
Ibrahim Matar
Jan Siemens
Mark Siemens
Julia Zanayed

Contents

Author's Preface — 9
Introduction by Frank H. Epp — 13

  1. Getting Oriented in East Jerusalem — 17
  2. The Promise of Camp David — 24
  3. Why the Palestinians Hesitate — 32
  4. Autonomy: Humiliation or Liberation? — 37
  5. Alternatives to a Palestinian State — 48
  6. Religious Conflict in Israel — 53
  7. Is There a Resurgent Islam? — 61
  8. The Ancient Churches Survive — 68
  9. Will Lebanon Survive? — 73
10. The Iranian Revolution — 81
11. The United Nations in the Middle East — 89
12. Five Pillars of the New Middle East — 96
13. Trying to Think Ethically in Jerusalem — 111

A Checklist of Topics to Consider in the Search for
      Peace Between Israel and the Palestinians — 117
Suggestions for Further Reading — 121
The Author — 123

Author's Preface

Foreign visitors to Jerusalem usually enter this ancient city from either the west or the east. Most foreigners fly into the Ben Gurion airport near the modern city of Tel Aviv and then drive on a new four lane limited access highway across the cultivated coastal plain and up the Judean mountains to "Jerusalem the golden." A small proportion of visitors come to Jerusalem from the east. These people cross the Jordan River bridge, drive through the oldest city on earth, Jericho, and up the arid hills of the Judean desert to Jerusalem. Visitors using the western portal feel like they are entering a modern, westernized city. Visitors from the east will see a much more traditional society.

These two ways of entering Jerusalem help to determine what one sees and how one views the human situation from Jerusalem. If one comes from the east, he will probably call the bridge over the Jordan River the King Hussein Bridge. If coming from the west, the same person will probably call it the Allenby Bridge. If traveling by taxi from the airport, the visitor will ride a "sherut" while the person at the bridge will ask for a "service." The "sherut" driver will want dollars or Israeli pounds. The "service" driver prefers dollars or Jordanian dinars. The person entering from the west will probably be impressed by the modernity and unity of Israel and Jerusalem. The person entering from the east, after passing several military checkpoints, will feel the disunity. And once in Jerusalem it is hard not to notice the striking difference between the flourishing night life of Jaffa Road, the main street of West Jerusalem, and the emptiness of Saladin Street, the main street of East Jerusalem.

On our most recent trip our family entered Jerusalem from the east. For the next ten months we lived in East Jerusalem, that part of the city which from 1948 to 1967 was under Jordanian administration separated from the larger "new" or West Jerusalem which became capital of the new State of Israel. The two cities were separated by a no man's land. After the war of 1967 Israel occupied East Jerusalem as well as the other parts of Palestine which were either under Jordanian (West Bank) or Egyptian (Gaza Strip) control. Jerusalem was presumed to be united. But the differing languages (Hebrew-west, Arabic-east), cultures (Israeli-Palestinian Arab), religion (Jewish-Islamic-Christian), and attitudes suggest that the unity is imposed, certainly not freely chosen.

The essays in this book were written in East Jerusalem between September 1978 and June 1979. While the point of view is my own, it will be apparent to all readers that this setting colors what is written here. But I was also an outsider so I can hardly speak for the people of East Jerusalem. I cannot claim to know these people well enough or to have lived there long enough to be an expert. Of one thing I am sure— that their point of view is not well known in North America. Their perspective may not be historically accurate or morally correct but it is a point of view that must be taken seriously if peace with justice is to be achieved in the Middle East. So I make no apologies for these views from East Jerusalem.

Nevertheless, as a person interested in the pursuit of truth and as one with a concern for human well-being, I have also tried to think in broader, less self-interested terms than the citizen of any city, including Jerusalem, is inclined to do. My own frame of reference is as an American academic and a pacifist Christian. I believe that faith and values ought to permeate not only action but analysis. Hopefully, this too will be apparent in what is here called *The View from East Jerusalem.*

Neither the single essays nor the total collection can be considered comprehensive in any way. Numerous important topics such as governmental organization, political parties, and the impact of inflation are not addressed here. The topics included are ones that interested me and which I believe are important in understanding the Middle East. In spite of the selectivity of issues and the limitations in scope, I hope this modest book will contribute to greater interest and deeper understanding of the contemporary Middle East, especially the conflict between Israeli and Palestinian. Most of all, I hope readers will understand how the conflicts in the Middle East involve the entire world and that all people, especially North Americans, ought to resolve to support the things that make for a peace that can truly represent the *Shalom* of Judaism, the *Salaam* of Islam, and the reconciled creation of Christianity.

Events come and go in the Middle East with amazing rapidity. Some of these essays may appear to be quickly dated. However, I hope the analysis can continue for some time to illuminate trends and suggest alternate policies that might be pursued in the continuing history of the region.

Persons interested in pursuing these issues further can begin with the reading list found at the back of this book. Since I present my material in essays rather than thoroughly researched documents, citations are limited to the few quotations cited in the text.

Many people have contributed to my understandings of the issues discussed in these pages. I will single out only the Jerusalem staff of Mennonite Central Committee to whom this volume is dedicated. Their friendship, hospitality, and gentle wisdom were important ingredients in making East Jerusalem such a pleasant place to live. I owe Goshen College the gratitude due an institution which in the face of changing academic trends and financial pressures has courageously maintained sabbatical leaves for its faculty.

While in East Jerusalem I served as a consultant to Mennonite Central Committee (MCC), a service and development agency at work there since 1950. MCC volunteers in Jerusalem, Amman, Beirut, and Cairo provided their own special insight and helped to arrange a variety of contacts with Middle Eastern people who enriched my life as well as afforded observations of greater validity.

Finally, I must mention the good offices of Herald Press who on short notice facilitated the prompt publication of this book. Chapters 6, 7, 9, 10 previously appeared in *Christian Living,* chapter 4 in *Christianity and Crisis* (April 20, 1979) in slightly different form and chapter 5 in *New Outlook* (September, 1979).

September 1979   *John A. Lapp*
                                        Goshen, Indiana

Introduction

This timely book clarifies various aspects of the Middle East conflict at a critical time. The author deals with recent developments and with neglected, little understood issues. In so doing he gives Western readers much-needed perspective from the other side of Jerusalem. This book should be read by everybody in the West who is interested in gaining a better understanding of this troubled area.

To be sure, to identify critical times in the Middle East is nothing new. Since the Great War at least, and especially since the State of Israel was proclaimed in 1948, the area has known no peace as one crisis followed another. The wars that were fought ended not in peace settlements but only in so-called cease-fires. If only the firings had ceased, but they didn't!

Except in one area. Since President Sadat's historic visit to Jerusalem in 1977 a new relationship has developed between Israel and Egypt, with the promise of a permanent peace on Egypt's eastern flank and Israel's southern border. In that sense the times are less critical than once they were.

However, the peace treaty between the two most power-ful states in the area, reducing substantially the possibility of another full-scale war, has focused world attention on the conflict between Israel and the Palestinians. This dimension of the conflict was always the most fundamental and critical, though somehow the quarrel between Israel and the various Arab States always overshadowed, indeed hid from view, the fact that the Palestinians were also at war with Israel. The Palestinians have never accepted their ongoing displace-ment from their land. The military occupation by Israel since 1967 of the West Bank, East Jerusalem, and Gaza has become totally unacceptable.

A variety of factors have now made facing the Palestinian question unavoidable. These include the peace accords between Israel and Egypt, the worldwide recognition of the Palestinian plight as a human rights issue, the backing of their cause by Arab states now made rich and powerful by oil, American dependence on that oil, the resurgence of Islam as a significant force, the continuing carnage in Lebanon as a consequence of the Palestinian displacement, the increasing miserableness of the military occupation, and the effective international political work of the Palestinian Liberation Organization (PLO), including their high-level persuasions at the United Nations.

For Israel and the world Jewish community the issues are thorny ones. Israel made peace with Sadat and surrendered the Sinai on the assumption that the pressures would lessen and that no more territorial concessions would be necessary. For Israel complete and permanent sovereignty over all of Jerusalem, West Bank, and Gaza is not only a question of se-curity but one of national ego and of a people's identity and self-understanding.

Thus, quite unexpectedly the long-awaited "peace" in the

Middle East has brought all the parties in the Middle East conflict to the heart of the matter. Unless resolution of the most basic and central issue—the conflict between Israel and the Palestinians—is reached soon, the Middle East could experience a conflagration such as it has not yet known.

And not only the Middle East. The West (the United States in particular) is also approaching a moment of truth. Empathy for the Jews and the desire to make Israel secure contradict the need to allow the Palestinians their own state. Human rights and oil make the issue inescapable. No time dare be lost in securing Israel, while at the same time ending the military rule of occupied territories and peoples.

Failure to do so soon will result in further dilemmas of decision-making too difficult to contemplate. In the end, the oil shortage could result in once more turning Jews into national and international scapegoats and in Israel losing its best and strongest friend, the United States of America. This must not happen, and that is why the times are so critical and why the West must understand correctly and act wisely.

John Lapp's excellent book should be immensely helpful toward that end. His interpretation from East Jerusalem provides a perspective most of us in the West don't know as well as we should. By focusing on the events since 1977 he gives us what is most immediately relevant for the completion of "the peace process."

The author helps us understand such complex issues as Islam, the revolution in Iran, the meaning of Jewishness in Israel, the struggle in Lebanon, the role of the United Nations, the strange behavior of the Palestinians, and why the Arabs have rejected the Camp David accords. He does so, not by avoiding the complexity of issues or by oversimplifying them, but by explaining in language understandable to the lay reader the issues in all their complexities.

The View from East Jerusalem reflects the strengths of the academic scholar and the practicing journalist, of thorough research as well as experience in the field, of understanding and of compassion. Lapp, a history professor, spent his sabbatical in Jerusalem not only to write a book but also—and this is much more important at this point—to help end the conflict which "has sapped the spirit of millions and distorted the priorities of a generation of Arabs and Israelis."

Those who share his passion for peace can hardly do better than to pursue their quest with the help of this fresh, readable, update on the Middle East situation, an analysis of the contemporary situation not likely to be found in the media or in official government pronouncements. It cannot be recommended too strongly.

> *Frank H. Epp*
> Conrad Grebel College
> Waterloo, Ontario

CHAPTER 1

GETTING ORIENTED IN EAST JERUSALEM

To the outsider, Jerusalem appears as one city. But it doesn't take long to discover that the capital of ancient Judea and modern Israel is a complex mosaic of different quarters and neighborhoods. East Jerusalem with a population of nearly 100,000 is mostly Arab, but 35,000 Israelis live in large apartment complexes in what was once Arab-owned land. About 15 percent of the Arabs in East Jerusalem are Christian, the rest Muslim.

West Jerusalem has a highly variegated population of over 250,000, though the population is largely Jewish. One major division is between the religious and nonreligious Jews. Even more diverse is the rich ethnic mixture among Jewish Israelis whose ancestry is either Palestinian (probably from Jerusalem), European, or Oriental (coming from Morocco, Iraq, or points between). Of the 3.2 million Jewish Israelis slightly over half are Oriental, while the rest are mostly from Eastern Europe.

These population differences are accentuated by political, economic, and cultural differences among both Arabs and

Israelis. The really unique people among both population groupings are the minority who can claim to be Jerusalemites. Some families—Jewish, Christian, Muslim—can trace their Jerusalem addresses back hundreds of years. The significant fact today is that, like most non-Western cities, most Jerusalem residents are first-generation citizens. This is an ancient city with a new population.

Jerusalem in its complexity is a microcosm of the entire Middle East. The Middle East mosaic of fifteen nations from Morocco to Iraq and from the South Yemen to Syria encompasses a land area nearly the same size as the United States, but with one third as many people. Although a vast land area, 90 percent of the terrain is desert, a decisive ingredient in determining cultural styles.

One must make exceptions to every generalization about the Middle East. Here are some of the complexities of this fascinating geographical region: religious diversity within Islam, Judaism, and Christianity; political divisions; ideological disagreements; rich versus poor within and between nations; ethnic, linguistic, and religious minorities; the cultural continuum from village localism to metropolitan globalism; the economic continuum from dependent refugees to the highest national per capita incomes in the world; the violence continuum utilizing the most sophisticated ultramodern weaponry between states to the knives and clubs of a village feud; rapidly growing populations and a massive movement to burgeoning cities; declining public services in Egypt and Lebanon and growing services in Jordan and the gulf states; the division of the Palestinian nation between those in Israel, the occupied territories, and the diaspora; the outward emigration of peoples, especially the educated upper classes and Christians; the revolutionary amassing of wealth from petrodollars and remittances from overseas workers/supporters; the role of Israel geographically in the Middle East but culturally and economically part of the West; the variety of cultural traditions often in conflict—ancient, modern, and post-modern, Middle Eastern, African, Asian, and European; historic and often rival claims to holy places and holy lands; psychological alienation built on centuries of conflict, but especially because of the recent thirty-year Arab-Israeli war; distortion and misunderstanding bred by propaganda and prejudice; the revived interest in religiously motivated politics and politically inspired religion; tensions created by the cold war fought by surrogates and allies.

If complexity is one problem to encounter in understanding Jerusalem and the Middle East, a second one is cultural distance. To get inside the cultures of this region means learning new languages, especially Hebrew and Arabic, and learning another set of cultural patterns. Most of us in the West are outsiders to the religions of this region—Islam, Judaism, and eastern forms of Christianity.

But perhaps the most difficult problem Westerners have in understanding this region is the profound heritage of anti-Semitism all of us in Western Christendom have to a greater or lesser degree suffered from. One stream of this anti-Semitism is well known and need only be mentioned here—that is, the systematic ways in which from the early Christian epoch Jews and Judaism have been proscribed and sometimes criminally destroyed. It is important to remember that the Zionist movement within Judaism was in part an attempt to preserve Judaism in the face of European attacks. Israel itself was established in the aftermath of World War II and the Nazi attempt at the systematic destruction of European Jewry.

Less well known, but I believe just as critical, is the other profound anti-Semitism, namely the centuries long attack on Islam, the Arabs, and the systematic way this tradition and these people have suffered at the hands of the West, especially Christendom.

We are only now beginning to understand the many ways in which Islam, the Orient, Arabs, and Palestinians have been the victims of prejudice, distortion, stereotyping, and sheer ignorance. We need spend little time lamenting North American parochialism. Recent surveys suggest the situation is even worse than we might have thought. According to a U.S. Department of Education Survey of 1976 high school seniors, 27 percent thought Golda Meir was president of Egypt and 40 percent consider Israel an Arab nation! A Gallup poll in 1977 reported that over 50 percent of the American adult population did not know that the United States needed to import oil!

How easy it is for the American press to use labels when Arab peoples are mentioned. Terms such as "reactionary," "barbaric," "regressive," and "fundamentalist" were freely used to describe the opposition to the Shah in Iran. "Black robed mullahs" are presumed to be unlearned with an aversion to the West and wanting to "escape from modernity."

Such distortions have a long history which is certainly not one sided. Muslims are assured in the *Koran* that they "have become the best community ever raised up for mankind, enjoining the right and forbidding the wrong and having faith in God." Like the Chinese, Islamic peoples are told they are "a people in the middle" with the world revolving around them. But with the decline of the Ottomans in the eighteenth century, Islam lost self-confidence and prestige as well as power and influence.

The history of Western prejudice includes attitudes born in the clash of the Eastern and Western churches, nurtured by the Christian-Muslim conflicts of the tenth to seventeenth centuries, and continued in the epoch of Western imperial control. Terms like "fanatical," "cruel," "despotic" shade into "irrational," "picturesque," and "terrorist."

Edward Said in an article, "The Idea of Palestine in the West" (*Palestine Digest*, November 1978), points out how the Palestinian in our time brings into sharp focus 1,500 years of cultural stereotyping. He quotes Chaim Weizmann, Reinhold Niebuhr, and Edmund Wilson to illustrate the condescension and denigration that reach a climax in the famous aphorism, "a land without a people for a people without a land." Hence an Arab politican in Nazareth can say, "We are the Red Indians of Israel, the invisible people." The clash of Israeli and Palestinian today is but the most recent expression of a cultural conflict which often becomes a violent confrontation. Said concludes that Palestinians in the West continue to be abstractions but "tomorrow they will become actualities, not because they were not in fact actualities before, but because the West must concede that history is more than Western history."

This then is the setting in which we must try to understand the Middle East, especially the conflict between Israel and the Palestinians. It doesn't take long in Jerusalem to discover the fundamental issue—one small land (10,000 square miles) is claimed by two peoples. Israel today has a population of 3.7 million including 500,000 Arabs. The additional Palestinian population includes 750,000 living in the West Bank, 450,000 in the Gaza Strip, and about 1.5 million, mostly refugees, living in Jordan, Lebanon, and Syria.

Throughout recorded history Arabs (Christian and Muslim) and Jews have lived in Palestine. The modern clash between Israeli and Palestinian began with the emigration of Jews to Palestine which began in the 1870s. The British who ousted the Turkish rulers in 1917 promised European Zionists a homeland in Palestine. During the 1920s Palestinians began to protest the increased immigration. When the British could not or would not resolve the conflict and announced their withdrawal, an international struggle between Arabs and Jews broke out. Before the United Nations partition plan could be implemented the ill-prepared Arabs were defeated and the State of Israel was established.

Since 1948 almost perpetual conflict has continued between Israelis and Palestinian Arabs. Major wars erupted in 1956, 1967, and 1973. During the 1967 war Israel occupied an even larger territory and dominated the Palestinian Arabs who remained in Palestine. While the Israeli army has maintained its supremacy, the Arab armies showed considerable strength in the 1973 conflict.

The United Nations and the major world powers have tried a variety of approaches toward a peaceful resolution of this conflict. But each attempt has broken down over the basic issue—the right of one people to return to a homeland exercised at the expense of another people's right to live in theirs. Meanwhile, the Palestinians have organized a powerful political and military campaign designed at least to gain their own state, if not their entire homeland.

It is in this context that the year 1977 is pivotal in understanding present developments. Three things happened that year setting in motion dynamics not yet fully resolved.

The first of these, in March, was the decision of the Palestine Liberation Organization under the leadership of Yasir Arafat to agree to participate in a peace conference which included Israel. Up to this time the Palestinians had refused to recognize the validity of the Israeli state and hence refused to participate in any such negotiations.

The second event was the May election of a new prime minister of Israel, Menahem Begin. Begin was a leader of the Irgun, a revolutionary commando force during the 1948 war. Since then he led those groups within Israel most interested in expanding the frontiers of Israel and maintaining a strong military force. His election signaled enormous change in Israel. For the first time in thirty years the broadly based Zionist Labor Party was replaced by a coalition known as the Likud.

The third and perhaps the most significant event of 1977 was the visit of President Sadat of Egypt to Israel, including East and West Jerusalem, from November 19 to 21. This dramatic act by the most important Arab leader was the first overt recognition of the reality of Israel by an Arab statesman. Though Sadat spoke vigorously for the Palestinians, he broke the united front of the Arab rejectionists and, by implication, lent his hand to a two-state solution of the two peoples now living in Israel-Palestine.

Everything since has been groping in darkness and sometimes jockeying for power in working out the implications of these three very major events. The essays that follow explain why bringing this process to a conclusion has been so difficult.

CHAPTER 2

THE PROMISE OF CAMP DAVID

Whatever else it is, Jerusalem is the city most intimately involved in the Camp David accords of Presidents Carter and Sadat and Prime Minister Begin. If these agreements are to succeed, the people of Jerusalem—Arab and Israeli—are the ones who will put content into the "Framework for Peace in the Middle East."

Two basic agreements were made at Camp David in September 1978. "The Framework for a Conclusion of a Peace Treaty Between Egypt and Israel" is a relatively straightforward agreement that returns the Sinai Peninsula to Egypt with the withdrawal of Israeli occupation forces. The treaty signed after many delays on March 26, 1979, called for the transfer of authority to be completed within two or three years. Israel agreed to abandon its Sinai airfields and eighteen civilian settlements. Egypt proposed construction of a highway between the Sinai and Jordan across Israel territory, guaranteed Israel free passage in its territorial waters, and promised full diplomatic recognition (including freedom of travel and trade) to Israel and its citizens. United

Nations forces will be stationed on the borders to insure that the borders are demilitarized and the agreements not violated.

The second agreement provided for a "Framework for Peace in the Middle East" and is much more complicated and imprecise. Here Egypt and Israel invite other parties to join them in the search based on "the sovereignty, territorial integrity, and political independence of every state in the area" and "the legitimate rights of the Palestinian people and their just requirements." Specifically Egypt, Israel, and Jordan and representatives of the Palestinian people will be the major negotiators of this agreement. The transition would take place over five years during which the Israeli military government would be withdrawn and a self-governing authority established through elected representatives. Israeli forces, however, would remain deployed in "specified security locations." Joint Israeli and Jordanian patrols would presumeably "assure the security of the borders." No later than the third year negotiations would take place to determine "the final status of the West Bank and Gaza . . . and to conclude a peace treaty between Israel and Jordan."

This agreement is open to considerable interpretation. First of all Jordan was not party to the Camp David accords and has not agreed to participate in the negotiations. The timetable that is established allows for substantial changes in governments and public opinion. The Palestine Liberation Organization (PLO) headed by Yasir Arafat is not part of the process, although representatives could conceivably join the Egyptian and/or Jordanian delegations. Israel has not promised to evacuate the West Bank and Gaza, the one thing that is absolutely essential to the Palestinian position The status of East Jerusalem and the Israeli settlements are not mentioned except that Israel is not to expand or plan ad-

ditional settlements. Even here there are differences
between the Israeli interpretation and the American-
Egyptian understanding.

Public opinion in Israel has overwhelmingly supported
these accords and the Knesset (Israel's legislative body) has
strongly endorsed the government's action. But it is also
clear that relinquishing a major piece of territory and giving
up a substantial investment in settlements has created a
powerful undercurrent of unease throughout the country.
The prospects of additional territory being relinquished to
an independent Palestinian state means that even the
potential for peace involves a major upheaval in the Israeli
consciousness.

Until now Israel has not really had to think about limits.
The Zionist dream of a Jewish State co-extant with the *eretz
Israel* (land of Israel) has always been bigger than even the
present borders of the state. The growth of the Jewish population and the ensuing expansion of settlements before 1948
and the Arab-Israeli wars has contributed to a growth
psychology. So strong has been this drive that Zionists
developed the myth of an empty land waiting for colonists.
As recently as the early 1970s former Prime Minister Golda
Meir insisted there were no such people as Palestinians.

Expansion has been underscored by the conviction, primarily among the Orthodox citizenry, that the territories occupied since 1948, Judea and Samaria, are the real home-
lands of the Jews. Towns like Hebron, Bethel, Shilo, and
Shechem (Nablus) mean much more to the pious believer
than Natanya, Acre, Ashkelon, even Tel Aviv.

No one felt or promoted this point of view more than the
Likud coalition, now the major ruling group and Prime
Minister Menachem Begin. In 1969 Begin led his Herut
party out of the coalition government rather than face the

prospect of giving up the conquered territories. Begin has obviously conceded on this matter. Most of the opposition in the Knesset, however, was from the prime minister's own party—including the resignation of one cabinet member. Considerable infighting continues within the Likud as it faces up to the reality of being party to a peace they have always opposed.

Apart from the religious significance of the territories, the other argument for maintaining this land is for security reasons. Israel is small. From Dan on the northern border to Beersheba on the south is only about 200 miles. It takes less than two hours to drive across Israel from the Dead Sea to the Mediterranean. And so the military has pressed for space as a defense requirement. Israel's military has tended to be responsive to civilian control, partially because the political leadership like Foreign Minister Dayan and Defense Minister Weizman have earned their reputation in the military. Dayan especially has strongly promoted Israeli settlements in the territories as a means of strengthening control of the area. But it took a major struggle, including overruling the army chief of staff Rafael Eitan, forceably to remove illegal Gush Emunim settlers on a hilltop near Nablus in March 1979. If additional force is necessary to prevent future settlements or remove settlers to the pre-1967 borders, a major confrontation between military and civilian sectors could well take place.

But as Uri Avnery says, "The one thing more important to the state of Israel than property is peace." This longing is deeply felt by all sectors of Israeli society. The possibility of finally being able to operate as a part of the Middle Eastern community of nations has meant that most Israelis, in spite of their recent history, are ready to give up territory. The real question remains whether that longing for peace is powerful enough to result in taking the next steps of coming to terms with the Palestinians.

If Israel has fundamentally to decide between peace or territory, the Palestinians have to ask whether a vague commitment is enough on which to build a state. Until now Palestinians have almost uniformly said "no" to the Camp David agreements. The PLO participated in a meeting of "rejectionist" states in Damascus announcing their disapproval. In a series of meetings on the West Bank attended by mayors, lawyers, and students, the prevailing mood has been "absolutely and completely rejecting." Even the relatively moderate and pro-Jordanian mayor of Bethlehem, Elias Freij, asks, "Who is Sadat to negotiate for us?" Others say, "The West Bank needs no negotiating. It belongs to us already. The Camp David summit was a ploy to trick our leadership."

These attitudes come from a variety of sources. One is shock, simply because they were unprepared and also because they trusted Sadat not to negotiate a separate peace. (Sadat insists that Egypt will persist in future negotiations to uphold the Palestinians' position.) Most of all, Palestinians simply don't know what the accords really mean. Jordan's King Hussein, by no means a friend of many Palestinians, nonetheless asked their questions in a letter to President Carter: "What is the geographic definition of the West Bank? What sovereignty will the new state have after five years? Will the self-government authority be extended to East Jerusalem? What happens to Israeli settlements ... during and after the transitional period? What solutions are projected to the problem of Palestinians who have been living as refugees since 1948?"

Palestinians who have watched and waited are not inclined to try to fill in a framework. They have on several occasions both in Beirut and on West Bank said they would be prepared to accept the reality of Israel upon a total Israeli withdrawal from West Bank, Gaza, East Jerusalem, and the Golan Heights. Palestinians, both before and since Camp David, have not seen enough substance in the search for peace to become wholehearted participants. In their despair they haven't seen Camp David as hope, but as a sellout.

American analysts such as Joseph Kraft and Anthony Lewis, as well as some American diplomats, think the spirit of the agreements emphasizes the "transfer of authority" from Israel to the Arabs. According to this point of view, a local government with "full autonomy" would be in control on location. From that base a Palestinian state could develop that Israel could not prevent. Palestinians who have never ruled themselves have not yet generated the self-confidence or the foresight for this possibility.

The Palestinians are also part of a larger Arab reality. The Arabs are not united in their attitudes toward the Camp David treaties. The rejectionists—Syria, Iraq, and Libya— appear unable to adjust to a new reality. Egypt obviously is prepared. The imaginative leadership of President Sadat beginning with his November 1977 trip to Jerusalem set in motion the treaties now being discussed. Other Arab states— Jordan, Saudi Arabia, and Kuwait—appear ready to join the peace process if a Palestinian state stands a chance of becoming a reality. But constructively involving Jordan and Saudi Arabia will be tricky since both kings feel they have been bypassed by Presidents Sadat and Carter.

Specifically Saudi Arabia, the homeland of Mecca and Medina, sees itself as the core Arabic state and the preserver of Islamic orthodoxy. When the Saudi airline invites people to fly to the "Holy Land," they mean Arabia not Palestine! Saudi wealth has kept Sadat's Egypt afloat since the debacle of 1967 when the Suez Canal was closed. Saudi Arabia has funded other Arab nations, including the Palestine Liberation Organization. Partly this is because of the tradition of Muslim generosity toward the poor, but also it is an obvious way to influence regional politics. Money provides stability which in turn contributes to security. One of the keystones of Saudi interest is the return of East Jerusalem to Arab control. Jerusalem ranks next to Muhammad's home cities in the hierarchy of Islam's holy places. But none of the Camp David agreements even mentioned Jerusalem. King Khalid felt betrayed both by President Sadat and by President Carter. Much of what else has happened follows from this basic afront.

Saudi feelings of isolation have been increased by events in Iran. Not only was there a community of interest between the Shah and the Saudi monarchy, but also each was linked to the American alliance system. The Saudis perceived a weakness on the part of the United States in failing to more strongly support the Shah and hence have begun to look elsewhere for diplomatic and military links for their security. All of this is critically important for the region and the world because the Saudis have worked hard to preserve peace and unity in the Arab world to a great degree as the regional representatives of the worldwide superpower, the United States.

In spite of these difficulties the current negotiations between Egypt and Israel are the most hopeful steps toward peace since the establishment of Israel in 1948. The final big hurdles are the acceptance by the Palestinian Liberation Organization of the reality of Israel, and the readiness of Israel to withdraw from the lands it has occupied since the 1967 war. Both these actions require extensive reformulations of self-understanding by both sides. Israel will need to recognize that her own national security is bound up in the good will of the Palestinians rather than in a permanent state of hostility. The Palestinians will have to discover that freedom is not to be found in denying the existence of Israel but in cooperation with the Israeli people.

CHAPTER 3

WHY THE PALESTINIANS HESITATE

In Jerusalem the response to Camp David was severely muted. Israelis wondered what the implications of the peace are for a state that has only known war in the thirty years of its existence. Palestinians glumly continued to anticipate a long struggle until they achieve what they consider to be their rights. The people most intimately affected—the Palestinian Arabs who live in Jerusalem, the West Bank, and Gaza Strip—have also rejected the proposal, even though Israel for the first time formally recognized their existence, their "legitimate rights," and allowed for the development of a "self-governing authority." The official voice of the Palestinians, the Palestine Liberation Organization (PLO) has been most articulate in their response, but nearly everyone in the occupied territories has been equally adamant. Trying to understand this reaction ranging from outright rejection to only hesitant exploration of the possibilities for a settlement can be a helpful insight into the many sides of the Middle East tragedy.

One, the Palestinians have been shocked by the very fact

of these agreements. They have endured the humiliation of occupation and the intransigence of the Israelis so long that any agreement has appeared impossible. After more than thirty years of perpetual conflict, violence itself achieves a sense of normalcy. The biggest shock, however, was what is perceived as the lack of support for their cause by the biggest Arab state, Egypt. Since the formation of the Arab League in 1944 the essence of the Palestinian case was based on a common Arab front vis-a-vis Israel. Sadat has now broken ranks and the Palestinians feel weakened if not betrayed and abandoned.

Two, the Palestinians are unsure what the Camp David accords really mean. The accords provide a "framework" which includes Jordan and "representatives of the Palestinian people." Jordan has not agreed and who the representatives of the Palestinians might be is unknown. The extent and timetable of the Israeli military withdrawal is unclear. Numerous dimensions of the occupation are not mentioned. Indeed, the three parties at Camp David have in some cases had three interpretations of certain phrases and assumptions. The Palestinians had previously announced their own conditions for negotiation. One of these called for total Israeli withdrawal from the occupied territories. Even this expectation is not guaranteed in the Camp David accords.

Three, the Palestinians were not party to the negotiations. Can they really think of themselves as a self-conscious, self-determining people if other powers, especially the oppressor Israelis, now presume to determine their destiny? The framework requires translation and interpretation. How can the most immediately affected people respond enthusiastically if the accord appears as a *diktat*? Future participation is welcomed in the accords but the framework

may be so fixed, or their influence so weak, that in their own
mind such a role might be only ineffectual window dressing.
Israeli violations of the Geneva Convention regulations regarding captured territory have been conspicuous. Palestinians cannot understand why they should trust Israeli
promises now.

Four, the agreements do not guarantee a role for the PLO
in the negotiations. Indeed the language can be interpreted
to recognize any group except the PLO. Having experienced
the attempt by Israel to develop its own Palestinian party
and representatives, the bulk of the people suspect a new attempt to divide and rule. How, they ask, can there be a bona
fide Palestinian government which does not cope with the
reality that nearly two thirds of all Palestinians live outside
Palestine. The 1976 elections of West Bank mayors clearly
demonstrated the preference for the PLO within as well as
outside the occupied territories.

Five, the agreements do not specify what will happen to
the enormous Israeli investment in the West Bank and Gaza.
Here the beginning and end is the question of the many settlements and extensive building projects, especially in East
Jerusalem. If Israel does really move completely out of the
Sinai then the Palestinians might expect a similar
withdrawal in Gaza and West Bank. The move from the
Sinai hasn't taken place yet and, indeed if it does, Prime
Minister Begin says it should not be seen as a prototype for
the entire territories. During the past eleven years Israel has
systematically tried to integrate the occupied territories into
a united *eretz Israel* for the benefit of the Israelis, not the
Palestinians. Hence the insistence that justice requires a
return of the land and an evacuation of the buildings to
provide space at least for the return of the refugees.

Six, Palestinians are afraid the agreements do not

guarantee the return of East Jerusalem to Arab control. Even though Prime Minister Begin once said Sinai was a holy mountain never to be returned to Egypt and has obviously reneged, Palestinians know that much more emotion surrounds this unique city. Many, if not most, Israelis (let alone the Prime Minister) have declared that Jerusalem will never again be divided.

Seven, the Palestinians hesitate to respond to Camp David because they are a divided people. These divisions are geographical: between those in the West Bank and Gaza; between those in the occupied territories and those in the surrounding states. The Palestinians are divided ideologically: between rejectionists who can never accept the reality of Israel and those who accept the fact of Israel and might try to negotiate a settlement; between those who support a strong Jordan connection and those who want as little a connection as possible. Not the least damaging aspect of the long Israeli occupation has been the sustained prohibition of political activity in the villages and towns along with a not-too-subtle attempt to develop a network of collaborators.

Eight, the Palestinians are not sure that they have human resources for the risks of negotiation. Palestinians have never ruled themselves as an organized state. Though they are a highly talented people, their spirits have been bruised, their hopes disappointed so many times, their property exploited and often expropriated. Many of their most capable leaders have suffered imprisonment and exile. The end result is the domination of fear and distrust. Accepting Camp David, no matter how inadequate, requires a style and spirit that hasn't been part of their recent historical experience. The Palestinian revolution is still in the process of maturation.

There are, no doubt, other reasons why the Palestinians hesitate to accept the possibilities presented by the Camp

David agreements. In spite of these reservations, there is some evidence that small clusters of Palestinians will decide that Camp David presents the best alternative available. This group may even gain enough self-confidence and influence to enter a slate for the promised elections. The victors might then join the negotiations. Then the issue will no longer be Palestinian hesitation but the reality of the Israeli commitment to a "just, comprehensive, and durable peace."

CHAPTER 4

AUTONOMY: HUMILIATION OR LIBERATION?

Two vignettes from the occupied territories suggest the issues at stake in the negotiations between Egypt and Israel, with an American presence, regarding the Palestinian future.

On Monday, March 26, the day Menahem Begin and Anwar Sadat signed their peace treaty, the usually bustling villages and towns of the West Bank from Jenin in the north to Hebron in the south shut down to mark a "day of national humiliation." Shops and offices closed, much public transportation halted, to protest a treaty which "not only does not offer us anything, but also ignores the Palestine Liberation Organization." The *Jerusalem Post* indicated that this was "the largest general strike since 1967." The quieted streets of Old Jerusalem even lacked the ubiquitous tourists who were steered elsewhere for fear of an outburst of violence. But this action remained nonviolent and impressive in its totality.

Two days later on March 28 El Arish, the capital city of Sinai, burst with joy to celebrate its promised liberation before the middle of June from Israeli military occupation.

Nearly the entire town of over 40,000 people poured into the streets on buses, in trucks, and by foot to praise Sadat, Carter, and Begin. The following day when I visited this ancient caravan city, Egyptian flags continued to adorn houses, shops, and taxis. A large banner across the main street announced, "We will give our lives for Anwar Sadat." Mayor Ahmad el-Tanger, confined to bed for nearly a year recuperating from a stroke, celebrated the occasion by taking his first steps. He talked glowingly about the happiness of his city and its brighter future. He was most excited by the prospects of an early reunion with his three sons living in Cairo whom he has not seen since 1967. The priest of the local Coptic community eagerly solicited funds to clean his church building and light up its cross for the pending visit of President Sadat and Prime Minister Khalil.

Humilitation or liberation are two alternative responses to the painfully developed proposals for peace in the Middle East. The one treaty between Egypt and Israel insures the withdrawal of Israel from the Sinai and the return of Egyptian rule. The people of El Arish call this liberation. The second document, "Framework for Peace in the Middle East," envisions a process leading to "full autonomy to the inhabitants" of the West Bank and Gaza. During a five-year transition period negotiations will "determine the final status and its relationship with its neighbors and conclude a peace treaty between Israel and Jordan." Until now West Bank and Gaza residents interpret autonomy as humiliation. They too want liberation. The successful general strike underscored the unanimity of Palestinian opinion which every serious observer has noted since the Camp David accords were first announced. The only mayor on the West Bank elected in 1976 without PLO support, Elias Freij of Bethlehem, expressed his rejection of the treaty as vigorously as any nationalist, calling the accords a "legalization of Israeli occupation" wholly unacceptable to anyone in the territories.

The unanimity and vigor of this reaction has certainly disappointed both Egyptian and American negotiators who knew that no peace can be achieved without including the Palestinians and their "just requirements." Secretary of State Vance expressed the hopes of many that the Palestinian people will see these treaties and the negotiations now beginning as a "historic opportunity." Why then this rejection? Can the Palestinians possibly be wooed to join the peace-making process?

The Palestinians, as is well known but sometimes forgotten, are divided into three main categories. About 500,000 live within the pre-1967 borders of Israel and are known as Israeli Arabs. About 1.2 million live under Israeli military occupation in Gaza and West Bank. About 1.5 million live in Jordan, Syria, and Lebanon—some in refugee camps but many in the towns and cities of these countries. While any solution leading to peace will require the involvement of at least the latter two groups, this analysis emphasizes the point of view of those living under the occupation.

Even within the occupied territories there are subtle differences of opinion between those living in Gaza and those living in West Bank and between accommodationists and rejectionists. Forces within and without the community attempt to accentuate these differences. Since Camp David, however, Palestinians wherever they are located and whatever their ideological commitment agree that the Camp David formula inadequately defines the prerequisites of a just peace settlement.

Palestinians individually and in several statements signed by political, professional, and religious leaders have clearly expressed what they consider the basis for a just solution. At the West Bank National Conference held on October 1, 1978, in Jerusalem one hundred leaders put their case succinctly:

> No peace is possible in the area without the complete and genuine withdrawal of Israeli forces from all the occupied territories, nor without securing for the Palestinian people the right of return, self-determination, and the creation of their own independent state on their land, with Jerusalem as its capital.

These four basic demands have been set forth at numerous times and places. But here the occupied people themselves speak. It can probably be said that the "Framework for Peace" does not deny any of these expectations: total withdrawal, self-determination, independence, or Jerusalem as capital. It is equally true that none of the four are explicitly promised. Most West Bank people do not object to a transition period. What they fear is that these prerequisites for peace will be emaciated by the negotiating process and that the Israeli definition of autonomy will prevail. They are deeply disappointed that East Jerusalem is not mentioned in the Framework although they know it was the subject of heated debate at Camp David.

The Gaza National Conference which met on October 16 and 18, 1978, expressed the same desires as the West Bank leadership. As in the former statement, the weaknesses of the Camp David document were attacked vigorously. They cited violations of the U.N. charter, General Assembly resolutions, and the failure to recognize "the PLO as the sole and legitimate representative of the Palestinian Arab people." Most basic, however:

> The agreement entrenches Israeli occupation for an un-

limited period of time, endows it with legality, disrupts the
unity of the Palestinian people at home and abroad . . . and, in
addition, does not specify the removal of the settlements in the
West Bank and Gaza.

It is impossible to understand the strident tones of opposition to the Camp David agreements without recognizing
that these are the responses of a dominated people. Mayor
Mohammed Milhem of Halhoul observes that "we are sus-
picious because of our experience with Israel over the last
eleven years." To overcome the suspicion the Palestinians
will require more than vague promises that their goals might
be realized.

Yet since Camp David, Palestinian suspicions have
increased rather than relaxed, the opposite climate necessary
to create a context conducive to negotiation. These suspicions have been increased by Israeli actions. Instead of the
promised freeze on settlements publically announced by
Carter and Sadat, Israel moved ahead with the confiscation
of 1,200 acres of land from the village of Anata and 4,000
acres from the village of Abu Dis. In addition 100 acres from
the town of Hebron and 250 acres from the town of Beit Sa-
hour were closed, preventing new building and requiring
residents to have permits to enter their own houses. This
land has all been used by Palestinian farmers and much of it
was owned by them. In each case the expropriation or
closures include the houses of many families. The Gush
Emunim, though a private group, has called for new settlements in addition to the Nahals (paramilitary outposts) established during the months of January and February 1979.

These actions have been supplemented by a steady
stream of statements from the prime minister of Israel
promising additional settlements in Judea and Samaria
where Israel will always be sovereign. The most vigorous

proponent of settlement, Minister of Agriculture General Sharon, also chairs the cabinet committee on settlements. He insists that autonomy in the territories will not prevent additional settlements. In several speeches and interviews Sharon has expressed the need for additional land expropriations. "This is the proper time," he said in *Ma'Ariv* (January 26, 1979), "to make the decisions and to begin to carry them out in the field: seizure of lands, construction of water projects, paving of roads, fire areas for training, a broad military infrastructure." He promised thirty-two new settlements in 1978-79 and expects an ultimate population of 50, 000 Israelis in the West Bank alone. Presently about 8,000 Israeli settlers live on the West Bank and 35,000 in East Jerusalem.

More recently General Sharon and others began to emphasize the need to maintain control of water in the territories lest autonomy lead to Israel's being "dried out." Water is indeed an issue in a semi-arid region like Israel, Gaza, and West Bank. And without a doubt one of the most notable Israeli achievements has been its exploitation and development of the water resources. In the territories, water resources are not nearly so well developed. The critical issue for the West Bank is that already the 8,000 settlers (out of 750,000 people in the West Bank) are using a disproportionate amount of the water available. In 1977-78 the Israeli settlers used 14 million cubic meters out of a total 43 million cubic meters of water pumped. According to the Israel Water Authority the territories use on the average 20 cubic meters of water per head while Israel uses 60 cubic meters per head. Since 1967 Israel has dug 25 deep wells in the territories primarily for Israeli use and has not allowed Palestinian farmers to develop any new water sources for irrigation purposes.

Aggressive Israeli development, not to speak of confiscation of land and water resources, suggests to Palestinians that by the end of the transition and even before a self-government can be fully established their land and water will no longer be under their control. But then Begin has clearly defined autonomy as self-government for people, not for territory.

Similar suspicions are aroused by the continued attack on political freedom and civil liberties in the territories. For six weeks after Camp David some limited amount of freedom for political meetings and discussion was allowed. When it became apparent that opinion was strongly nationalistic, the military government withdrew this freedom. Similarly, since November 1978 repression on university campuses has increased with more extensive use of curfews and censorship. Indeed, in December collective punishment was revived in the form of demolishing a house where young men and women were suspected of participating in resistance activities.

This repression reached a high point in the weeks preceding and following the March 11-13, 1979, visit of President Carter. Primary, secondary, and university classes were suspended by the military governor. The Arabic press had more white space due to censorship than at any time since March 1976. Six persons were shot including two killed by soldiers firing into crowds of demonstrators. The town of Halhoul, after suffering the death of two young people, was under military curfew preventing any entrance or exit from the town for two weeks.

The distinguished Israeli writer Amos Elon recently wrote that "we rule the people against their will by violent means." This reality more than anything else has alienated the vast majority of the Palestinians living under Israeli rule.

These same people have heard the Israeli government state that the source of authority in the autonomy will continue to be the Israeli army without any guarantee of political and personal freedom or the sanctity of Palestinian property. Hence the mayor of Ramallah, Karim Khalaf, can say, "The autonomy plan is worse than the continued operation of the military government. . . . Today I know I'm living under an occupation and my rights as a subject . . . are more or less anchored in international law." In the autonomy, Khalaf says, the "military will have to rule by gunpoint."

Given this rejection of the Camp David treaty can we expect anything other than an imposed peace? Can an imposed peace have any future? Is there any chance that Palestinians, at least in the territories, might yet send some representatives to join the Egyptian delegation at the negotiating table?

In Jerusalem there are few signs of hope. Some Gaza and West Bank residents, however, even though eager for an independent state, are ready to say that the restoration of Egyptian and Jordanian rule as experienced before 1967 would be preferable to continued occupation and military domination. This is one clue that a note of desperation may be entering the nationalist camp. Another clue is the suggestion that just as the PLO signaled before the April 1976 municipal elections that nationalists should run for office and that the populace should vote, so as distasteful as the "Framework for Peace" appears, some Palestinians may join the negotiations simply to salvage the best deal possible at this moment. No Palestinian, except the isolated but usually well-known cooperator, has any confidence in the present Israeli government. Yet in spite of considerable displeasure with the American role in these negotiations, the United States continues to have a positive reputation on the West

Bank. If this prestige or power were properly used, it is quite likely that some Palestinian leaders with PLO support would join the negotiations. What are some of the signals that could entice Palestinians to participate in the next round of negotiations?

It is unlikely that such a signal can openly contradict present Israeli policies such as having the PLO itself nominate Palestinian representatives for the negotiations. President Carter, Secretary of State Vance, Senator Robert Byrd, and others have repeatedly called Israeli settlements on the West Bank and Gaza obstacles to peace and illegal according to international law. However, the unwillingness of the administration to put teeth into that position likely means the most that can be said in this regard is that there should be a freeze on settlements until the negotiators can speak to this issue.

From a number of soundings in the West Bank, it appears that reputable Palestinian leadership could be attracted to the negotiations with a clear statement by the American president on what he expects in the self-governing authority envisioned at Camp David. Such a statement must specify that power in this new entity will be derived from the inhabitants through the electoral process. It must specifically call for the complete withdrawal of all Israeli military forces to the 1949 armistice lines (many Palestinians are prepared for a demilitarized homeland under some international police force). It must insist that the new governing authority has title to the public domain lands in these territories with power to guide the development and allocation of land and mineral resources. Finally, such a statement ought to address the problem of Jerusalem which like other plural societies could remain physically united under two governing bodies.

Other important considerations are also necessary if this

self-governing authority is to be credible, legitimate, and
supported by Palestinians. What is spelled out here are the
kinds of provisions that will give Palestinians the feeling that
autonomy can be liberation and not humiliation.

The implications of such a statement should be quite
clear. It will mean that the new government will restore
lands confiscated from Palestinian villages and farmers during the past twelve years. Many Palestinians who lived on
the West Bank and Gaza before 1967 will want to return.
This is the primary reason why most Israeli settlements will
need to be dismantled unless some arrangement can be
made for the return of 1948 refugees to Israel in exchange
for Israelis becoming citizens of the new Palestinian state.

Other issues will be part of the extensive negotiation
process. These will include the precise location of borders;
freedom of movement between Gaza and the West Bank as
well as open borders with Israel; joint development of transportation and communication facilities; a timetable for the
transfer of authority and the establishment of the new
bureacracy.

The Framework for Peace in the Middle East is called the
basis for a "just, comprehensive, and durable settlement."
This remains a possibility if the core people, the Palestinians,
become a party to the negotiating process. But for them to
join the process their "legitimate rights" must be treated as
more than words. Israel can no longer claim sovereignty in
Judea and Samaria when it has clearly agreed both in U.N.
Resolution 242 and in signing this framework to "the inad-
missibility of the acquisition of territory by war." The
essence of the debate over autonomy is a question that can
no longer be postponed. Is autonomy genuine home rule or
occupation under another rubric?

The people of Gaza and the West Bank want more than

anything else liberation from the humiliation, demoralization, and oppression of the occupation. The Israeli military government's attempt to generate mutual respect and political dialogue has foundered on a combination of repressive actions and indigenous nationalism. The failure of military rule, Gaby Shefer of Hebrew University has written, is clinched by the fact that "there is not the slightest chance that the majority of the Palestinians would support 'autonomy' as a permanent solution."

The thirty-year Israeli-Palestinian war has not only destroyed many lives and resources. It has sapped the spirit of millions and distorted the priorities of a generation of Arabs and Israelis. The announced public positions of both Palestinians and Israelis leave us with a few grounds of hope in spite of the enormous energies expended in this most recent search for peace. Another chapter in this process can emerge if autonomy is seen as a step toward liberation and not a continuation of Palestinian humiliation.

CHAPTER 5

ALTERNATIVES TO A PALESTINIAN STATE

As Egyptian and Israeli negotiators continue to work on new governing arrangements for the West Bank and Gaza, territories occupied by the Israeli army since 1967, Prime Minister Menahem Begin speaking for a broad Israeli consensus has ruled out one possible outcome—a Palestinian state. The prime minister on several occasions, and the cabinet-approved proposal for autonomy, emphatically state that "there will never be a Palestinian state" in Palestine. Indeed, the annexes to the Israeli proposal specify that at the end of the five-year transition Israel expects to hold "full sovereignty over these territories."

The forthrightness of Israel's position on statehood underscores what is also the primary concern of the Palestinian people and makes it the central issue of the negotiations. Palestinians within and outside the territories are prepared to cooperate in a transitional government called autonomy if in the end they achieve statehood and sovereignty of the people in their own land.

One wonders what the alternatives are to these public

positions. For Palestinians these are obvious. Without statehood Palestinians will continue to live under occupation or as refugees in strange lands. What is less well recognized are the alternatives Israel must weigh as it opposes any Palestinian state in West Bank and Gaza. Before looking at these alternatives, Israel should also reckon with the fact that by vigorously opposing any Palestinian state it gradually loses whatever influence it may have in the equally important discussion on the kind of Palestinian state that could conceivably emerge.

One alternative to a Palestinian state would be for Israel to return the West Bank to Jordan and Gaza to Egypt with some minor border adjustments. This solution has been discussed primarily by Israel but has never matured because of Jordan's awareness of Palestinian national feeling, especially since the Rabat conference in 1974, and of the refusal of Israel to commit itself to withdraw completely to the pre-June 1967 boundaries. This alternative is not likely to emerge from the negotiations without a major change in position and strategy by the Palestinians. Those in Israel who might prefer this alternative should be aware that an enlarged Jordan with an overwhelming majority of native Palestinians would be a stronger state on its frontiers than a Palestinian entity based on the West Bank and Gaza. The repeated suggestion, most recently by Minister of Agriculture General Sharon, that Palestinians should take over the Hashemite Kingdom of Jordan is not only most unpolitic but portends the strongest kind of opponent in any prolonged Palestinian-Israeli confrontation.

The second alternative to a Palestinian state is even less likely. Yet there are a few Israelis and many more Palestinians who would like to see Israel transformed into a genuinely democratic state which disavows ethnic, religious, or linguistic privilege. Ever since the 1948 Declaration of Independence Israel has defined itself not only as a homeland for Jews but also as a Jewish State. There is no unanimity on what this means other than that the primary concern of the government is to provide security and well-being for its Jewish citizenry and a haven for Jewish people living anywhere. The secular state alternative would appear to be very remote given the present national consensus and the growing strength of the religious community within Israeli society.

This leaves a third alternative to a Palestinian state which is a continuation of military rule in the West Bank and Gaza. The substance of this alternative is based on the demographic fact of 3.2 million Jewish Israelis dominating not only 500,000 Palestinians within the pre-1967 borders but now an additional 1.2 million Palestinians in these territories. Another 1.5 million Palestinians are refugee exiles in the neighboring countries. The essential policy of the military government appears to be attempting to break down any notion of Palestinian cultural identity and societal organization. This means rigid control over cultural institutions like schools and the press. Population centers will be broken into smaller units by the presence of Israeli settlements and a network of roads so that a united Palestinian society no longer appears viable and formal annexation to Israel no longer necessary. The conspicuous evidences of military rule—preventive detention, house demolitions, town curfews, school and university closures, deportations, land seizures (out of 32,000 acres seized at least 28,000 acres have been privately owned) are the inevitable results of enforcing such a policy. The recent increase in vigilante activity by Israeli settlers is simply impatient citizenry implementing the official policy at a faster rate in a conspicuous style.

The reaction of the Palestinians under the military occupation has been sullen and often defiant. Their options are to forego self-determination, emigrate, or be forced from their homeland, brood, and complain about their fate sometimes like Langston Hughes's "Raisin in the Sun," or explode by throwing a stone, planting a bomb, or staging a demonstration. Virtually no forums for the public discussion of grievances or development of a Palestinian policy are tolerated by the military government.

Some may consider autonomy as a fourth alternative to a Palestinian state. But as envisioned at Camp David, autonomy would be a period of transition toward self-government and potentially statehood. The Israel prime minister on the other hand has described autonomy as a status where the Israeli military would control security. Palestinian self-rule would be limited to personal affairs and definitely not include control of their land and water resources. Defined thus autonomy is no alternative. It is simply a continuation of military rule.

There are three alternatives then to a Palestinian state. There would appear to be no others. (1) The West Bank, possibly joined by Gaza, could again become part of Jordan which portends an enlarged Arab power. (2) Israel might become a truly secular society incorporating all the people within the post-1967 boundaries into a genuinely democratic political order with all the implications for the concept of a Jewish state. Or (3) Israel can continue its military domination with its potential for international war, the certainty of internal tension, and the continuing militarization of Israeli society with the inevitable brutalization of its people.

There are no guarantees that an independent Palestinian state would be a model of civic decorum. Nevertheless, the psychological satisfaction of statehood in the West Bank and

Gaza might enable such an entity to become a responsible center for the fulfillment of their national aspirations. Just as Israel does not attract all Jews neither will all Palestinians choose to return to this land. Just as in Israel, however, there will be a law of return and a program for rehabilitating refugees. Many Palestinians are prepared to envision a demilitarized state with international guarantees. With reciprocal gestures such a state might become the link to a regional confederation involving Jordan, Israel, Egypt, Lebanon, and perhaps Syria.

The issues involved in the Egypt-Israeli negotiations are as critical for Israel as for the Palestinians. The alternatives to a Palestinian state have to do with the essence of Israeli statehood. Will Israel be a homeland for Jewish people and a center of social and cultural creativity? Or will Israel become an ever more fearful minority exhausting its energies in dominating another talented and inventive people?

CHAPTER 6

RELIGIOUS CONFLICT IN ISRAEL

It is impossible to be in Jerusalem and fail to see the Dome of the Rock, the Church of the Holy Sepulchre, or the Western Wall of the Temple Mount. Jerusalem is an important center to the three great monotheistic traditions—Judaism, Christianity, and Islam. Presumably united in the belief in one God, each of the three faiths is deeply divided ideologically, culturally, and politically. In this chapter I will focus on the disunity within Judaism in Israel.

Since December 1977 one major issue in Israel has been the Christian community's struggle to preserve the right of propagation and conversion in the face of legislative attempts to restrict freedom of religious expression to simply freedom of worship. Another continuing controversy involves the privileges and sanctity of the "holy places." In 1979 this issue centered on the Machpelah Cave, also called the Tomb of the Patriarchs, in Hebron. This tomb of Abraham and Isaac is sacred to Jews and Muslims both of whom have long used it for public worship. Since the Israeli occupation of the West Bank, Jews have pressed to restore their

worship rights which were abrogated between 1929 and
1967. The military authorities have negotiated certain time
periods and places in the large mosque for Jewish worship.
These provisions have not satisfied ultra-orthodox Jews who
want use of the total building and have pressed their cause
with petitions and demonstrations. Some Muslims suspect
these enthusiasts want complete domination or control.
Meanwhile the occupying army maintains an uneasy truce.

But the main religious controversies in Israel are not
between Jew and Christian or Jew and Muslim. Rather the
issue is the nearly continuous conflict that rages between the
various religious and nonreligious groups within Israel all of
whom stand in some relation to Judaism. The problem is
compounded by the fact that only one Jewish tradition—the
Orthodox, has official status. Here we will attempt to
describe and analyze this fascinating story generally unknown to non-Jewish North Americans.

One way to sense the dimensions of conflict is to list some
of the headlines which appear in Israel's main English language newspaper, the *Jerusalem Post* during the fall and
winter of 1978-79.

Basketballer's Conversion Raises Storm
Ritual Slaughterers Plan Hunger Strike
Agudat Yisrael Won't Join Coalition if Soccer Stadium Open on
*   Shabbat*
Curb Religious Zealots
Stabbing on Sabbath Riot
Kult Urkampf By Stealth
Rabbis Clash Over Sabbath Incidents
Sabbath Drivers Stoned Near Ramot
Religious Zealots Call for "Pray In" on New Ramot Road
Ramot Residents Warn No Religious Ghetto Here
Gush Emunim Settlers Forceably Removed From Nablus
*   Hilltop*

Play May Drop Curtain On Government Coalition
Deliberations Begun On Petition Of Jewess Who Believes In Jesus
New Bill On National Service For Girls
Kashrut War Threatens Knesset
Zealots Clash With Police Over New Capital Stadium

Newspaper headlines frequently distort the issue reported. The above are no exception. They do, however, indicate the scope and frequency of religious controversy. Every week and sometimes every day four to six separate stories in the press involve religious concerns. While there appears to be some increase in this struggle during recent months, it is also clear that the issues cited above are variations on themes that have rent Israel since its establishment thirty years ago. The major themes are legislative regulations regarding Sabbath observance, dietary restrictions, and military exemptions for ultra-orthodox Jews; the question of who is a Jew; marriage and divorce regulations; and boundaries of the land of Israel. Ethnic, linguistic, cultural, economic, and generational differences mean that none of these disputes can be defined in purely religious terms. Religious differences, however, focus the conflict.

The story of the Ramot Road that created nearly two months of Shabbat violence during the winter of 1978-79 illustrates the political dimensions of religion in Israel. Ramot is a new Jerusalem suburb northwest of the city built on some of the land Israel occupied after 1967. A new highway to Ramot was opened in December 1978. The one mile long, six-lane asphalt strip skirts very close to Kiryat Sanz, a small community of 400 orthodox families. These people moved out of the crowded Orthodox Mea Shearim section of the city beginning in 1965. This location was chosen because of cheap land located near the former green

line separating Israel from West Bank. Here these serious-
minded devotees could live God-fearing lives apart from the
distractions of the secular world.

The 1967 war ended their isolation even though other Orthodox suburbs developed close by. The new settlement on
the next hill used an old road which was separated from
Kiryat Sanz by an industrial park. The new road is between
the industrial park and Kiryat Sanz.

As soon as bulldozers began clearing a new path in 1976
the residents appealed to both city and national authorities
that this road would upset the religious "status quo" which
since 1948 has governed inter-Jewish relations in Israel. In
effect the so-called "status quo" said there would be no
upsetting of any religious prerogatives without some *quid
pro quo* arrangements for the parties involved. Now the
people of Kiryat Sanz say the isolation of their neighborhood
is violated, especially by traffic on the Sabbath. In many
towns and cities in Israel the Sabbath is strictly observed
with a variety of "blue laws," including the closing of some
streets. In West Jerusalem no public buses operate on Shabbat and over twenty streets are closed to traffic from sundown Friday to sundown Saturday.

Many of the extreme orthodox Jews are organized into a
political party called the Agudat Israel. This party is con-
tinually challenged by a smaller and even more rigid group
called the Neturai Karta. The latter group numbering only
in the hundreds do not participate in Israeli politics because
they consider the state of Israel illegitimate since the state
was established before the arrival of the Messiah. The Neturai, however, have demonstrated on occasion to express
their sense of grievance.

The mayor of Jerusalem in 1976 responded to the petitions and demonstrations, saying, "We will do our best to

see that drivers refrain from traveling on [the Ramot Road] on the Sabbath." The mayor even had the engineers try to find an alternate route which never proved feasible. So the road was opened in December and every Sabbath since then drivers who dared to use the road have had their cars stoned. Buses had their tires slashed in neighboring Mea Shearim. The people of Ramot, many of whom are totally secular and the rest who are less rigidly Orthodox, have organized their own militia to keep the arterial highway open. They have also threatened to unleash German shepherd dogs to clear the road for their use. The city council of Jerusalem, so far to no avail, has been trying to find a compromise solution. The religious ecclesiastical courts have refused to issue a judgment on the case.

The same kind of controversy permeates Israeli life at numerous other points. A recurring quarrel has been going on between Jerusalem hotels and the Rabbinate over sabbath observance by their employees. The Jerusalem Hilton was a special target since it had a catering contract for the national legislature (the Knesset).

Americans have been caught in the interreligious controversy recently in two interesting ways. Eileen Dorflinger, born of Jewish parents in Connecticut, came to Israel in 1976 as a new immigrant. She claimed citizenship based on the Law of Return which guarantees such a privilege to all Jews. Soon it was discovered that she was also a baptized Christian. This meant she was denied citizenship because she was not a Jew. She appealed to the High Court of Justice claiming, "I am a Jewess." The court held that Dorflinger, by becoming a Christian, was indeed no longer a Jew and hence not eligible for citizenship under the Law of Return.

Aulcie Perry is an American who went to Israel to play basketball for a professional team. Before emigrating Perry converted to Judaism at the "Tiferet Israel" in Brooklyn, New York. The problem for Perry is that this synagogue and its rabbi are not recognized by the Rabbinical Council of America. Hence Agudat Israel members in Israel refuse to recognize Perry's conversion as valid which also jeopardizes his citizenship. Both Dorflinger and Perry reflect the most devisive religious issue of all, "Who is a Jew?"

These current cases are the tip of what a Harvard historian of Egyptian Jewish origin, Nadav Safran, calls "the most complex, the most vexing, and potentially the most explosive problem bequeathed to Israel by Jewish history." Safran sees the conflict as "an irrepressible opposition between two segments of itself over an issue both consider vital." "How long," he says paraphrasing Abraham Lincoln, "can a nation remain half-sacerdotal, half-secular?" This religious controversy is about the very identity of this nation-state.

It would be easy to exaggerate the size of this problem. At this moment, at least, these tensions are simply that. Safran estimates that at most 15 percent of the population want a theocratic state and about 30 percent want a secular state. He says that of the remaining 55 percent a substantial majority want some link between religion and the state but not as rigidly defined as the Agudat group.

Religious political parties, however, are able to exert influence far out of proportion to their size for three reasons. First, with the state defining itself as Jewish, those groups with well-developed notions of what Judaism means are bound to have considerable public appeal. Second, the religious parties have almost always been part of the ruling coalitions (for many years with the dominant Labor Alignment and currently with the Likud coalition). In a multi-party situation where governments are formed from a variety of parties a single interest group is able to exert pressure on the governing bloc for policies it especially wants. The Begin government's coalition was momentarily threatened earlier in 1979 when a theater in Tel Aviv announced Friday night performances. The National Religious Party said "No" which forced Begin to pressure the Tel Aviv city government to refuse permission to the theater. In August 1979 Begin asked Mayor Kolleck of Jerusalem to postpone action on a new sports stadium in the suburb of Shufat because of Orthodox objections. They feared desecration of the Sabbath, protesting what they called the "Hellenization of Israeli culture."

A third reason why the religious parties have increased in influence if not actual power—it is well to remember that only ten to twelve Knesset members are elected by religious parties—is that as the earlier ideological underpinning of the national myth seems less attractive, the religious ideology continues strong. For instance, the early Zionists included a strong socialist program. As the state of Israel has developed, national security has become more important than social experiment. A religious rationale hence has been extremely influential in mobilizing national sentiment. Most recently religious factors have been used to justify the continuing presence of Israel in the territories occupied after the 1967 war. The Gush Emunim (Bloc of the Faithful) have organized paramilitary forces to establish settlements in these territories and have called for their annexation as the provinces of Judea and Samaria.

Zalman Abramov has entitled his excellent study of "Jewish Religion in a Jewish State" *Perpetual Dilemma* (1976). He notes that the issue is essentially unresolvable, for Jews "are at one and the same time a community of faith, as well as an ethnic national community." As a descriptive

statement for Israel this is certainly accurate, even though
most Jews in the world today live in religiously plural
societies. As circumstances and population ratios change in
the Middle East, definitions in Israel may also be forced to
change. A few Orthodox, especially those connected with
the Movement for Torah Judaism, feel Judaism in Israel has
become so politicized that the spirit is languishing. They
want a reformation by de-politicizing the faith. Until then
observers of the Israeli scene, like Israelis themselves, must
pay close attention to the religious factor in Israeli politics.

CHAPTER 7

IS THERE A RESURGENT ISLAM?

Living in Jerusalem one is impressed by the evidence of religious faith conspicuous everywhere. A major point of identity for most people, religion influences nearly every dimension of life. The "religious idiom," Mohammed Sid-Ahmed says, is "the salient mode of political expression through the region." This is particularly true in the Islamic Republic of Iran proclaimed by the Ayatollah Khomeini on April 1, 1979, but almost to the same degree in Saudi Arabia and Israel (with, of course, different faiths).

The triumph of Khomeini is only the most newsworthy of this new vitality within Islam. New mosques are being built; Muslim women are returning to traditional dress including the veil, some say in return for a stipend from the oil rich states of Saudi Arabia and Libya; abundant religious literature, much of it attractively produced, is available in a variety of languages; and frequent pictorial and oral references of public piety by public officials are circulated among the people. There is some evidence of new adherents to Islam in Central Africa and Central Asia. Saudi Arabia university students are required to take religious instruction during each of their four-year baccalaureate program.

The political expressions of this new vitality are widespread. Kings and parliaments vie with each other to reestablish Islamic law—*Shari'a*—as the basis of public law. Pakistan's President Mohammed Zia ul-Haq marked the Prophet Muhammad's birthday in February by announcing new punishments for crime based on the *Shari'a*. Iran is revising its banking code to reflect the teachings of the prophet that usury (interest) is sin. The new constitution in Iran will provide for a separate religious body to review, ratify, or reject governmental actions. In Egypt the Muslim Brotherhood, first established in the 1930s to lead a religious revival, is now much in evidence after being proscribed by President Nasser in the 1950s. This organization, active in a number of countries, controls the student organizations on all Egyptian university campuses. The same night President Carter accompanied Egyptian President Sadat to Alexandria in early March 1979, university students staged a demonstration protesting the Egyptian-Israeli peace treaty and praising Khomeini. The March 1979 issue of the Brotherhood magazine *Al Dawa* was confiscated by the government because it asked Egypt to join Iran in a holy war against Israel.

Like all great religions, Islam is made up of various subgroups. The most important division is between the Sunnis which prevail in the Arab countries and the Shi'ites who dominate in Iran. Another division is between the very traditional, uncompromising "fundamentalist Islam" and the modernizers who are prepared to adapt the tradition to current ways of thought and action. This resurgence is taking place in all groups and nearly everywhere within Islamdom from Indonesia to Morocco. Considerable tensions exist between the various groups and the attitudes they express.

An interesting conflict is taking place between the religious organizations of rigidly orthodox Saudi Arabia and President Kaddafi of Libya, generally known for his religious fervor. Kaddafi has suggested that some of the traditions of Islam were late additions and not as valid as those attributed to the Prophet himself. The Saudis have accused the Libyan of the heresy of individualism rather than accepting the consensus of the scholars and have asked him to repudiate his deviation. Just as interesting as the phenomena of revival is some understanding why revitalization occurs and why now. There is no one reason for this development. Each group and region experiences revitalization in slightly different ways.

First, any religion with staying power tends to experience moments of renewal and revival. Muhammad himself once said, "At the turn of each century there will arise in my nation a man who will call for religious revival." Individuals and groups will be gripped again with the reality of God (Allah) and submit anew to the message of the ancient teachings (Islam). Sometimes a prophet will emerge who will creatively apply the teachings to the contemporary situation. In the midst of enormous social change, people hunger for spiritual meaning and significance. In this regard the motivation fulfills an essentially religious search.

Politics are also related to most revivals. Here again we are dealing with a very Islamic phenomenon. From its establishment in the seventh century Islam has been concerned that its conscience permeate all of life. It sees political power as an appropriate vehicle for extending its influence. What is going on today in Pakistan, Iran, and Egypt is typically Islamic. Indeed, scholars like Kenneth Cragg say, "The political is the form in which Islamic self-consciousness expresses itself." What is so interesting is that though the religion appears conservative the politics can be revolutionary, such as the overthrow of the Shah. The Egyptian commentator Sid-Ahmed points out how this can happen. "The Shah brutally repressed every form of political opposition. Dissatisfaction and frustration could be expressed only in the name of the one authority the Shah dared not challenge: Allah." Nations which have suffered from colonial domination or international discrimination find religion a valuable medium for mobilizing opinion against external power and influence.

The third important cause of this resurgence is the new cultural energy within Islamic civilization. For at least the last three centuries Islamic countries have been retreating before the impact of the dynamic West and modern technology. This civilization once nearly dominant in Eurasia and North Africa has been bruised and insulted by the arrogance of the West. A kind of inevitable anti-Western bias in this movement is aimed primarily at what Muslims consider decadent, hedonistic culture. During the January 1977 riots in Cairo, the Brotherhood vented its anger on night clubs, movie theaters, and tourists hotels where this hedonism was most evident. The tension between Arabs and Israelis in Jerusalem often boils down to the insult that scantily clad young men and women are to puritanical Muslims. The Muslim way of life is working to cope with the impact of secular westernism by keeping novelty within a clearly Islamic framework. Indeed the presence of Israel within Islamdom is considered to be an affront which in turn has helped stimulate this resurgence. (Jewish pressure for worship rights at Muslim holy places such as the Tomb of Abraham in Hebron and on the Temple Mount in Jerusalem threaten to turn the Palestinian-Israeli conflict into a massive religious struggle.)

An important ingredient in this new cultural energy is the burgeoning wealth of the oil rich Islamic states. Beginning in 1970 when the OPEC nations usurped the power to set the price for crude oil, the Islamic states have been amassing enormous wealth. Saudi Arabia now has monetary reserves of over $35 billion, second only to West Germany and far outdistancing the United States and Canada. An Egyptian, non-Muslim professor says the cultural impact of this wealth is seen by Muslims as proof of "divine intervention on our side."

This mixture of wealth, status, political influence, and religious meaning, although varying from place to place, is the force motivating the revival that is at hand.

Considerable disagreement exists over the significance of this revival. One Lebanese Christian theologian calls the resurgence "a purely Western phobia" whose impact will be short-lived because it is a "reaction" rather than a positive indigenous force. Others, particularly Israelis, tend to see this resurgence as a "terrifying revival of fundamentalistic Islamic integralism." Muslims themselves, in the words of a Sunni professor at the American University of Beirut, consider Iranian developments as "creative and responsible." Palestinians in the occupied territories have seen in the Iranian movement a force that may help them in their liberation, but it is also significant that the strong Christian component within the Palestine Liberation Organization has reminded leader Yasir Arafat that his embrace of Khomeini doesn't suggest a "secular, democratic" ideology.

Whatever one's assessment, it is important to note that Islam continues to attract enormous support and provides meaning to millions of people. The tradition continues to be vital in spite of the difficulties in adapting Muhammad's teachings to the modern world. Any attempt to organize life

around submission to God and values of communal responsibility would seem to be preferrable to the pragmatic,
pleasure-oriented values of so much of modernity. Lebanese
Greek Orthodox Bishop George Khoder suggests that Islamic criteria for public life may be better than the "totalitarian, pseudo-socialistic, and ultra nationalistic."

One of the major problems the Islamic world has never
satisfactorily resolved is its treatment of minorities. Some of
these are Muslim and some are not. Among those most fearful of this resurgence are Jews in Iran and Israel and Christians in Lebanon and Egypt. Eastern Christians in particular
have been active in Arab nationalist movements as a way of
lessening the impact of Islam totalism. The largest Christian
church in the East—the Egyptian Copts—are the most fearful that the new power within Islam will upset their own ac-
commodation to Islam carefully worked out through centuries of relationships. The Copts strongly support Sadat
who has controlled Islamic enthusiasm for ten years. But if
the promised benefits of peace do not materialize, a vigorous
Islamic resurgence there could follow the pattern of the
Iranian revolution.

This resurgence presents a special problem for those of us
committed to the Great Commission of our Lord. How is the
gospel presented among peoples with highly developed religious consciousness? This book is not the place to spell out
an answer except to observe that one reason for the existence
of Islam and the Islamic resurgence is that the Christian
message continues to be seen as the enemy rather than as a
hope of liberation. This unfortunate linkage of Christianity
with the armies of imperial Rome and the oil companies of
the modern West has distorted the gospel and prevented a
genuine encounter with the incarnate Savior and Lord—
Jesus of Nazareth.

Perhaps the most unfortunate dimension of the Christian failure has been its denigration of Eastern peoples, especially Arabs, who Jack Shaheen says are now "TV's most popular villain." It is impossible to relate to people, particularly those with a well developed self-consciousness, who have been villified as reactionaries and barbarians. Perhaps the message of a resurgent Islam is that we must take more seriously the authenticity of other people and the reality of their faith. As Gil Carl Alroy has recently written in another regard:

> We ought to pay a little more respect to the fact that the Islamic world is not a cheap, poor, or inferior copy of ourselves. They are not better—they are not worse, they are themselves, and I think we ought to stop interpreting them as if they were backward copies of the Western world: it is patronizing and it is false.

CHAPTER 8

THE ANCIENT CHURCHES SURVIVE

It is a measure of our provincialism and ignorance in the West, as well as a lack of ecumenical vision, that we so often forget that the church has always been a part of the Middle Eastern mosaic. Indeed Jerusalem boasts almost as many church buildings as synagogues although there are many more mosques. Some of my most interesting experiences have been to visit the ancient monasteries which continue to survive in the remote valleys of the Judean desert.

Some ten to twelve million Christians live in the Arab world. More than 70 percent of these belong to the so-called ancient churches who trace their lineage to congregations founded during the Apostolic age. About 25 percent belong to Western churches—Protestant and Roman Catholic— which entered the region during the modern missionary epoch. The vast majority of these members come from families that in earlier times were part of the Eastern churches. For instance the Coptic Evangelical Church in Egypt grew out of the Coptic Orthodox Church as a result of the extensive work of American Presbyterian missionaries.

The Greek Catholic Church so large in Israel, the occupied territories, Lebanon, and Syria, though linked to Rome, continues to use the Orthodox liturgy from their long experience as Greek Orthodox Christians. The largest Christian groups in the region are Coptic Orthodox, over 4 million; Greek Orthodox, 1.2 million; Maronite Catholic, 500,000; Armenian Orthodox, 550,000; and Roman Catholic, 1.5 million. In addition there are Syrian Orthodox, 180,000; Assyrian Nestorian, 180,000; and Protestant, 200,000.

The ancient churches are organized into patriarchates. The patriarch is the bishop in a city where the church was presumably founded by one of the apostles. Hence Mark is venerated by Copts and Greek Orthodox as the founder of the church in Alexandria, James is honored by the Armenians in Jerusalem, and Paul is the patron of the patriarchate of Antioch now headquartered in Damascus. In summer of 1979 the only patriarch I ever visited with, Elias IV, died in Damascus. His memorable words, "If you want to really know me you must return to visit again and again," suggest that Christian fraternal relations require more than occasional visits or periodic church assemblies.

It is difficult to describe the character of the Eastern churches in a few paragraphs. Yet I will offer some general statements which I believe to be valid.

One, the title "Orthodox" is critically important. Not infrequently early in an encounter with an Eastern churchman the issue of one's beliefs or creed enters the conversation. Eastern churches since the third and fourth centuries have evolved highly developed systems of belief. And these systems continue to divide. Armenian, Syrian, and Coptic Orthodox historically have not accepted the Chalcedon definition of Christ accepted by the Greek Orthodox and Roman Catholic. The non-Chalcedonian Orthodox are

sometimes called "Monophysite," referring to the single nature of Christ with the divine absorbing the human. This
distinction, however, is rapidly breaking down in modern
theological thought. The Assyrian church emphasizes the
separation of the divine and human nature of Christ more so
than Chalcedon. Orthodoxy has been closely identified with
a highly developed liturgy. Here the entire drama of re-
demption—incarnation, death, and resurrection—is
reenacted with the worshiper caught up in the mystery of
the miraculous. It has been well said that the heart of
Eastern Orthodoxy beats in the act of worship, not in the
pursuit of the Christian way of life.

Two, these churches tend to identify with a national or
ethnic tradition. The Copts are Egyptian, the Nestorians are
Assyrians, and the Armenians are from Armenia. The other
patriarchates such as Antioch and Jerusalem are very Arab
although the higher clergy in the Jerusalem patriarchate are
Greek. The clash between the Arab membership and the
Greek hierarchy in Jerusalem has severely weakened this
church in recent years. The linkage of these churches to their
cultural tradition means that the label does not always mean
personal commitment. Hence the question of "who is a
Christian" in the Middle East is almost as important as "who
is a Jew" has become in Israel. Orthodoxy now needs to be
clarified.

Three, these are minority churches. Only in Lebanon can
one find a Christian majority, but even here the churches see
themselves as a minority in the context of the overwhelming
Islamic character of the Arab world. It is possible to be a
creative minority. Eastern Christians have played, and
continue to play, important roles not only in the worldwide
church but also within their own societies. During the
development of the Arab national movements Christians

were in leadership positions in Lebanon, Syria, Palestine, and Egypt. They have also been conspicuous in education, medicine, and diplomacy. But all too often these persons are quite secular so that the church and Christian values are foreign to their vocation. Pressure on these minorities is always present, sometimes in hostile actions by the Muslim majority, more frequently in the insecurities of second-class citizenship. The issue of church unity is not a luxury for minority churches but rather a requisite for renewed faithfulness.

Four, these churches are ambivalent about the worldwide church. These churches carry the heavy burden of having once suffered from the crusading church of Rome in the eleventh and twelfth centuries. Then they had to bear the burden of needing fellowship with other Christians which made them appear hostile to Islam. More recently these churches have lost members to the aggressive evangelistic techniques of Western missionaries. Certainly one reason Eastern Christians have strongly supported nationalist movements has been their eagerness to demonstrate their patriotism. This frequently has led to their hostility to Western imperial powers often closely linked with Roman Catholic and Protestant churches.

The greatness of the Eastern church has been its tenacious ability to survive in the face of enormous difficulties. And it has done more than survive. The rich variety of Orthodox iconography and liturgical forms have on repeated occasions stimulated the forms of worship throughout Christiandom. The devotion of Orthodox Christians to worship and prayer are a continual inspiration, especially to the worldly Christians of the West. The suffering of these churches are a reminder that Christ expected His followers also to carry a cross. Today the remarkable renewal movement in the

Coptic Orthodox Church has made it one of the most aggressive missionary forces in Africa.

During the recent turmoil in Lebanon and Iran, the church has frequently been in the center of the strife. In Lebanon, Armenian Christians have found themselves literally in the crossfire between Maronite Philangists and leftist forces largely Muslim but also with some Christians. In Iran we have yet to hear how the small Christian minority is coping with the vigor of the Islamic government.

The churches in the Middle East are also facing new attempts by the majority religious forces in Egypt and Israel to restrict religious liberty to worship rather than the possibility of inviting other people to join the Christian movement. The efforts of the various councils of churches to preserve religious liberty is presently one of their most important activities.

The Eastern churches want and need the fellowship of the church in the West. But this will only be valid and enriching if Eastern Christians are accepted fully as brothers and sisters in a common pilgrimage and recognized for the strength that comes from maintaining and extending the Christian cause for over 1,900 years. Then we might truly fulfill the hope of Gabby Habib, executive secretary of the Middle East Council of Churches and lay Orthodox theologian, who says the church East and West must demonstrate that "Christian power is not in money and politics but through the Holy Spirit, the power of the powerless."

CHAPTER 9

WILL LEBANON SURVIVE?

Since the end of the war in Vietnam, no other country in the world has had as torturous an existence as Lebanon. This little country the size of Connecticut began the decade of the 1970s with a population of over 3 million and with a thriving economy. In 1974 civil disturbances broke out which led to a nineteen-month civil war (April 1975-October 1976). The cease-fire breaks down periodically as it did in large outbursts in July and October 1978. Since none of the basic problems of Lebanese society have been resolved, more violence can be expected.

It is difficult to grasp either the enormity or complexity of what has happened to a country once known as the "Switzerland of the Middle East." During the nearly four years of hot and cold war some 60,000 people, mostly civilian, have been killed. Proportionally, this would be 75 times as many casualties as the Americans experienced during eight years of conflict in Vietnam. Five hundred more were killed during the heavy bombardment of East Beirut in October 1978. In addition some 500,000 persons have left the country—

most of the wealthy and much of the middle class.

During this time, physical damage is estimated at more than three billion dollars. Vast sections of Beirut, especially the east side, look like the bombed European cities of World War II. Lost revenues stemming from lost production, absence of tourists, and interrupted trade are estimated at up to $50 billion. Public transportation and communication have become paralyzed. What freedom of movement there is depends on the daily fluctuations of local control.

Saddest of all is the fatalism that permeates much of the populace. With the breakdown of law and order, private armies and occupation forces provide the stability, such as it is, that prevents total anarchy. Even so, the thievery, looting, blackmail, assassination, and kidnapping between rival groups underscores the absence of a central governing body. In no other country have the pronouncements of governing officials been ignored so routinely as in Lebanon since 1975.

The story of the civil war reflects the fragmentation of Lebanese public life and the ever-shifting political alliances. Hostilities commenced between conservative and liberal groups in April 1975. During the course of this conflict the Palestinians (500,000 of whom live in Lebanon as refugees) were gradually drawn in. The Palestinian involvement precipitated Syrian intervention, which in early 1976 helped to keep the conservative groups from being overwhelmed. By the time of the October 1976 ceasefire 30,000 Syrian troops were stationed in Lebanon. This uneasy truce broke down repeatedly with the most violent eruptions in 1978.

The conservative forces, mostly Maronite Christians, decided their future lay only in a smaller state where they would be in control. The Syrians then began to shift their support so the 1978 conflict was largely between the conservative secessionists with the Syrians supporting the central government's struggle to maintain a united country. The prospects are gloomy. As one Beirut editor observed, "Here we are with three armies, two police forces, 22 militias, 42 parties, nine Palestinian organizations, four radio stations, and two television stations."

Before looking at the various strands in this civil war, it is important to reckon with several significant features of Lebanon. The first of these is the brevity of its existence. As an independent nation it is less than four decades old gaining its independence from the French in 1943. Second, though politically youthful, this mountainous coastal region has long been culturally unique. Usually governed by whatever power controls Damascus, Lebanon nevertheless has looked westward during most of its history. The strong presence of Maronite Christians and occupation by Crusader chieftains limited the power of various Arab and Turkish rulers. France since the seventeenth century has had a close commercial and religious tie to the port cities of Tyre, Sidon, Tripoli, and more recently Beirut. Nevertheless, Lebanon has always been considered an integral part of the Arab world. Indeed, in many regards it is the intellectual and cultural capital of the Arabs now divided into the states of Syria, Iraq, Jordan, Palestine, and Saudi Arabia. Throughout Arab history there has been tension and competition between the northern sector—the states mentioned above—and those centered in North Africa, where Cairo and Egypt served a similar role. Finally, it must be underscored that Lebanon has never really been united. Indeed, the so-called "national covenant" which structured political life since 1943 is based on each major group having a guaranteed place in the government. The Maronites, then considered the largest political entity, were given the presidency; the Sunni Muslims, the prime ministership; the Shi'ite Muslims, the presidency of the chamber of deputies. To maintain this fiction, no census has been taken since 1932, even though the Sunni Muslims are now assumed to have a larger population than the Maronite Christians.

Disunity and instability are inherent in the fact of Lebanon. In the 1970s what is implicit became explicit so that even President Sarkiss on Independence Day—November 22, 1978—observed, "Lebanon is disintegrating in front of our very eyes." The forces of disunity, he added, "engulfed the life of the world's happiest people with bitterness and misery." What then are these forces?

First and foremost is a society built on powerful family, clanlike units. Prominent among the Maronites are such family names as Chamoun, Edde, Franjieh, and Gemayel. Among the Sunni Muslims the names Karami, Salaam, and Al-Solh dominate. The conspicuous Druze minority has been led by the Jumblatts. These eight families have supplied most of Lebanon's presidents and prime ministers. Today each is part of the shifting alliances of the civil war.

Second, there are religious tensions. The majority of the largest Christian group—the Maronites—tend to oppose the Muslims not so much out of religious differences as in a struggle for power and influence. The Maronites are Roman Catholic followers of St. Maron who lived in Syria in the seventh century. Since the seventeenth century they have been struggling for autonomy as an independent political entity. Actually, the Maronites today are divided. Followers of Chamoun's National Liberal Party and Gemayel's Phalangists are pressing for an autonomous state, while the Franjiehists are now working for national unity, especially since Tony Franjieh was assassinated by Phalangists in July 1978.

The other large Christian groups—Greek Orthodox,

Greek Catholic, and Armenian—generally support a strong central government. Many of them would like the covenant of 1943 revised so their constituents could also achieve national political power. The Armenians, because so many live in East Beirut, have suffered enormously for their attempt at remaining neutral throughout the conflict. Muslims and Druzes are also divided and rarely act as single power blocs.

Although the Lebanese conflict is not primarily between Christians and Muslims, it is possible to understate the religious conflict. Early in this century nearly 100,000 Maronites died from Turkish persecution at the same time as the notorious pogroms against Armenians were underway. Maronites have some justification for their fear of being submerged in an overwhelming Islamic society. This potential adds a shrill note to Maronite propaganda.

The third source of disunity is the great gulf which separates the wealthy, many of whom are Christians, from the impoverished masses who are mostly Muslim. In this context much of the Lebanese wealth has been spent defending the status quo. Some additional wealth has also gone into sophisticated writings pretending to demonstrate that the real Lebanese are Phoenician rather than Arab. But far more goes to support ultra-conservative and reactionary political parties and private armies. The Phalangists, dominated by the Gemayel family and the National Liberals of the Chamounists, are united in a Lebanese Front now manning the barricades in East Beirut and the port city of Jeunieh. On the other side are the forces which minimally want to preserve national unity. The left, led by the Druze chief Walid Jumblatt, wants an end to freewheeling Lebanese capitalism and the creation of a socialist society. The left also has its militias.

The fourth source of disunity is the presence of 500,000

Palestinians with their many factions. The sheer size of this foreign element, one sixth of the total population, has upset the uneasy equilibrium that Lebanon maintained earlier. The alliance of the Palestinians with the Lebanese left and the retaliation of Israel to Palestinian commando operations adds to the tension. The civil war really began over this fact and the nature of the Palestinian presence. Since the 1976 truce, however, the main Palestinian forces of the PLO have tried to stay out of the conflict.

Finally, there are the international dimensions of Lebanese disunity. Already mentioned is the tension between Cairo and Damascus for dominance in the Arab world. Wherever a left-right battle springs up one can assume the cold war political involvement of the United States and Russia. For the most part, however, this has not been a primary cause of the tension. Another important international factor is the influence of the overseas Lebanese. This group which is largely Christian supplies much of the funding for the Lebanese Front.

The most important international dimension of the situation in Lebanon is the influence of the neighboring states of Syria and Israel. But their involvement is also very complex. On the one hand Syria has never forgotten that Lebanon was once part of the province of Syria under Ottoman rule. The Greater Syria movement includes Lebanon in its concern to unite all Syrians. Indeed, most Lebanese families have relatives living in the present state of Syria. Since the autumn of 1976 the 30,000 Syrians have been the mainstay of the Arab deterrant force trying to maintain the uneasy cease-fire. Saudi Arabia and Sudan also provide troops for the deterrant force.

Israel's involvement is also complex. Southern Lebanon, at least up to the Litani River, has often been considered part of Greater Israel. But actual Israel involvement in Lebanon began in retaliatory raids against Palestinian guerrilla camps. At the same time Israel has been promoting the idea of independence for all minority groups in the Middle East based on the idea of a "community of faiths and communities." Hence Israel became a chief source of arms for the Phalangists. As many as 1,500 Israel military "advisers" have been helping train Phalangist militia. Meetings have been held between Israel leadership and Lebanese Front leaders. Since the Israeli invasion of Lebanon in March and April 1978 there have been close working relations between the Israeli military and "Christian" militia who now control the Lebanese region immediately next to the Israeli border. While the Israeli army withdrew after the 1978 invasion, Israeli planes continue to fly over Lebanon daily and frequently bomb presumed Palestinian military positions. There are also continued commando operations in Lebanese territory.

No prediction about Lebanon is safe to make. Knowledgeable Lebanese expect more violent eruptions. There will be an attempt to disarm the private militias as well as the Palestinians. These people assume the central government, with Syrian support, will survive and that some kind of national unity can be reestablished.

Yet this seems a little glib given the profound forces that have torn this little country apart. I rather think that a reconstituting of Lebanon will require some fundamental changes in the body politic. At minimum this will require: 1. A solution to the Palestinian question so the refugees can either return to their homes or be resettled elsewhere. 2. The developing of a politics based on secular principles rather than a politics built on personal relationships or a vaguely defined religious identity. 3. Overcoming the large gaps between rich and poor and the equalization of public services. 4. A guarantee to respect the integrity and freedom of all religious and ethnic groups.

These changes are hardly revolutionary in a Western context. In the Middle East, however, they represent a social order not achieved in any other country. In this sense Lebanon continues to be the pacesetter in the region. The Lebanese Civil War could be the critical stage in the development of the region. It might also be the foretaste of endemic violence that could engulf the entire region, if not the world.

CHAPTER 10

THE IRANIAN REVOLUTION

As in most countries the Israeli press centers most of its attention on domestic affairs. Because of the dependence of Israel on American political economic and military support there is also considerable coverage of American affairs. But events in Iran during the revolution leading to the ouster of the Shah were followed carefully in the Israeli press.

And with good reason. Iran under the Shah was the only Middle Eastern country that maintained diplomatic ties with Israel. There was an extensive trade between Israel and Iran. Many items such as frozen chicken and fresh eggs were resold by Iranian traders to the Arab states of the Persian Gulf who formally boycotted Israeli products. One important dimension of the Iranian Revolution was the severing of diplomatic and commercial ties between Iran and Israel. More than that, the new government of the Ayatollah Khomeini welcomed the Palestinian leader Yasir Arafat, the enemy of Israel, and openly supports the establishment of a Palestinian state.

The flight of the Shah in February 1979 came after nearly

a year of open confrontation between the people and the ruler, also known as "King of Kings" and "the shadow of God upon earth." During 1978 upwards of 5,000 people were killed in the military's attempt to squelch the protest. By January 1979 the students said, "Your guns and tanks don't scare us." The turmoil brought about a virtual halt to Iran's massive oil production. The end result has been a standstill in the drive to create in Iran the world's fifth largest industrial and military power. The army, bulwark of the Shah's regime, was deeply divided. Increasing numbers of troops refused to fire on demonstrators, finally joining the opposition and supporting the new government. A new government formed by Mehdi Bazargan has been established but the power behind the throne is clearly the Ayatollah Khomeini and his mullahs.

What happened to this absolute monarch who ruled with conspicuous splendor and celebrated 2,500 years of the Persian monarchy in a $20 million extravaganza in 1971? How did it happen that in a country where the only openly organized political life was beholden to "His Imperial Majesty Shah Mohammed Riza Pahlavi," the government could be humiliated by unarmed students and workers crying, "Allah is great, death to the Shah"? Why should a country increasing in wealth and power reject the "White Revolution" of the "Shah and the People" for the traditional religious leadership, the Shi'ite mullahs? While we do not yet have complete answers to these questions or even know the final outcome of this turn of events, enough has transpired to suggest that what has taken place can be labeled "the Iranian revolution."

Like most Middle Eastern societies, Iran is deeply entrenched in traditional patterns of life and thought. Eighty percent of the 35 million people live in some 50,000 villages.

Most of this peasantry is closely attuned to the soil, which they work for several hundred landowning families. The villages are dominated by landlords who stand at the top of a well-graduated society. The villages and landlords tend to belong to large family and linguistic groupings. Less than one third of the people speak the national Persian language. The most important tribe is the Bakhtiaris. It was no accident that the person who tried to organize a civilian government before the Shah went into exile was one of the leaders of this clan—Shahpur Bakhtiar.

Most of the people are Shi'ite Muslims led by leaders called mullahs. (Iran is the only Muslim country with a Shi'ite majority. Shi'ites follow the Prophet Muhammad's son-in-law, Ali, and through the years have developed rituals and dogmas different from the majority Sunni Muslims.) As in other Middle East countries there is a close link between religion, politics, and society. Indeed Shi'ite Islam is as much a part of the Persian identity as Sunni Islam characterizes most Arabs.

In this traditional context the Shah, after solidifying his power in the 1950s, decided on a vast enterprise of modernization. In 1962 he decreed the "White Revolution," a series of reforms which would change Iran from a poor, traditional, inconsequential country into a wealthy, urban, modern, regional power. The basis for such a transformation was the income derived from the sale of oil and industrial products. The revolution would include land reform, nationalization of forests, publicly financed but privately owned industry, a literacy campaign, developing political opportunities for women, and a health corps. Such reforms were initiated by decree and administered by a bureaucracy appointed, directed, and promoted by the Shah.

The oil price increases of 1973 gave the Shah new incentives to push harder his development plans. Describing his "great civilization" which would be "one of the five industrial powers [after the United States, Russia, West Germany, and Japan] before the end of the century," he ordered a doubling of national investments in the 1973-78 development plan—from $36 billion to $69 billion. When some of his advisers told him this could not be done, he replaced them saying, "The secret of success is to systematically defy the advice of technocrats."

By 1976, with general inflation over 40 percent per year (and inflation for rent over 100 percent), numerous bottlenecks to the "revolution" were appearing. It was simply impossible to train people fast enough for the skills needed for high technology. Of the 100,000 students studying overseas each year, less than 3,000 a year returned to work in Iran. Iranian ports were not big or efficient enough to handle the growing imports. Desires far out ran the agricultural capacity so that the nation which was self-sufficient in food during the 1960s became an importer during the 1970s. An enormous gap between the rich and the poor emerged, no longer based on a landed aristocracy but rather on a new bourgeoise. The richest 10 percent of the population consumed 40 percent of the goods. Corruption became a way of life for the administrators of bloated national budgets. Half a million peasants left the villages each year, most to live in the expanding slums of the cities.

The Shah has always believed he ruled by "divine appointment." "The White Revolution" was considered "the creed of the Shah." He told Oriana Fallaci in 1973, "I believe in God and that I have been chosen by God to perform a task." To insure that his dreams and decrees were carried out he developed an enormous police system built around the army and a secret intelligence group called

SAVAK. Landowners who protested the breakup of their estates, mullahs who decried the hedonism of the new secularized culture, intellectuals who questioned the arbitrary use of power and the distorted national agenda were subjected to censure and imprisonment. One poet told the French journalist Eric Rouleau that "the choice forced upon us by the Shah is in reality a choice between renouncing one's beliefs or facing the firing squad." Political parties were proscribed, the press rigidly controlled. Amnesty International estimated that in 1974-75 there were between 25,000 and 100,000 political prisoners in Iran. "The Shah of Iran," they observed, "retains his benevolent image despite the highest rate of death penalties in the world, no valid system of civilian courts, and a history of torture which is beyond belief."

With oil revenues surging from $2.5 billion in 1971 to $20 billion in 1977, the Shah had funds not only to create new industry but also to pay for a glamorous army. Indeed as the oil consuming countries struggled for ways to pay mounting bills, they developed a market for weaponry. The United States sold Iran $10 billion worth of military equipment between 1971 and 1976 and $10 billion more was in the pipeline for 1977-82. France and Britain were in the market as well. The planes, tanks, destroyers, electronic communication, and warning systems are ostensibly to provide stability in the Persian Gulf and Indian ocean. The United States had a military mission in Iran since before 1950 helping train and direct the army.

Most observers, and certainly American officials, have been surprised that "the absolute ruler of a nation of critical strategic and economic importance to the United States is rather swiftly rendered powerless" (*International Herald Tribune*, Jan. 2, 1979). Yet there were clues for many years that the Shah, if not Iran, had feet of clay. After all, had not the Shah been restored to power in 1953 by the American CIA? And hadn't the regime of Dr. Mohammed Mossadegh, which took over the Anglo-Iranian Oil Company in 1951, evidenced a strong nationalistic outlook? Iranian students held protest demonstrations whenever the Shah visited the United States or Western Europe, which was not infrequently. Over a dozen Americans, military and civilian, had been assassinated in Iran since 1973 which surely said something. The number of persons in prison and in exile demonstrated the existence of a deep, if not extensive opposition.

Iran has had all the ingredients for a revolution for a long time—an arrogant ruler, an opulent irresponsible newly rich class, an ineffectual and corrupt bureacracy, an aggrieved old aristocracy, urban masses with rising expectations, a religious leadership concerned with preserving traditional values, and concerned intellectuals supported by large ranks of students.

By the fall of 1977 the Iranian economy was sputtering. An oil glut kept the price of oil down. The ports were jammed so that goods were not being distributed as rapidly as they should have been. One hundred and ten thousand resident foreigners (40,000 of them Americans) living as Westerners were a constant irritant to national sensitivities. All that was needed was a spark. Like most revolutions this one began with a clumsy action by the old regime. The long-outlawed National Front, which ruled Iran from 1951 to 1953, quickly seized the moment to direct the nearly spontaneous opposition.

In January 1978 a Tehran newspaper poked fun at the piety of an exiled Shi'ite mullah, the Ayatollah Ruhollah Khomeini. When religious students marched in protest, troops fired on them. From six to twenty students, depending on whom you believe, died. This set off a cycle of killing, mourning, demonstrations, and more killings that grew throughout the year. By June, parliamentarians were talking of new parties. When 400 people died in a fire set in a theater in Abadan in August, the tension mounted to new heights. Martial law was declared in September. One government was replaced with another. The Shah tried liberalization, freeing political prisoners, even confessing his failures. Then came a military government and a general strike.

By this time the exiled Mullah Khomeini was a national hero. The student movement merged with the religious opposition during the early days of December 1978. By the end of December, with the demoralized Shah lacking will or power, the bourgeoise joined the movement, and the troops in several cities joined the rebellion. The general strike closed the oil fields, ports, industry, newspapers, railroads, and airfields. Foreigners streamed out of town in an airlift. The Shah was denounced as "an American dog" and American business offices were firebombed. In six more weeks the Shah, a prisoner in his palace, decided to leave.

Like most revolutions, the upheaval in Iran has no simple explanations. It is too early to tell whether this revolution will result in substantial social and political change or abort. There are some who see here primarily a reaction against modernity, hence a counterrevolution rather than progressive movement. Others will emphasize the instability generated by external forces both Eastern and Western. The impact of these events disrupted the American alliance system, upset the triangular trade of Iran-Israel-South Africa, and threatened neighboring absolute monarchs in Jordan and Saudi Arabia.

To date what has transpired is deeply and authentically Iranian. Time will tell if it is also deeply and authentically revolutionary. The discontent of the leftists and the rebellion of the many minorities, especially the long unhappy Kurds, may become so powerful that the Ayatollah may not remain in power. Nevertheless, Iran in 1979 was surely different from Iran in 1977.

The Egyptian editor Mustafa Amin wrote an appropriate obituary. "He [the Shah] had given the people factories but had taken justice from them. He had given them a well-equipped army, but had denied them liberty. He had weakened all the men around him and none of them were now there to protect him."

CHAPTER 11

THE UNITED NATIONS IN THE MIDDLE EAST

Next to Israeli army equipment the most noticeable vehicles on Jerusalem streets are the numerous white motor vehicles painted with the conspicuous large black letters, UN. The license plates suggest more differentiated designations: UNEF (UN Emergency Force); UNTSO (UN Truce Supervision Organization in Palestine); UNDOF (UN Disengagement Observer Force); UNIFIL (UN Interim Force in Lebanon); UNP (UN Police); UNRWA (UN Relief and Works Agency); and UNFICYP (UN Peacekeeping Force in Cyprus).

In no other region in the world has the United Nations been so intimately involved. From the UN Special Committee on Palestine (UNSCOP) which recommended the partition of Palestine in November 1947 until the May 1979 meetings of Greek and Turkish Cypriots under the personal guidance of Secretary General Kurt Waldheim the UN has been on the scene. More time, money, personnel, policy-making and peacekeeping time have been devoted to the United Nations goal of international peace and security here than anywhere else. The headquarters of the United Nations in the Middle East is on a high hill south of Jerusalem which once served as headquarters for the British Mandate government.

Most of the work of the United Nations is unglamorous. Outside this region not many people realize how central United Nations activities are to the livelihood and stability of this region and indirectly of the whole world. What follows then is a survey of this positive contribution to world order.

Pope Paul VI over a decade ago coined the phrase, "Development is the new name for peace." The pope was highlighting the fact that peace is more than the absence of violent conflict. Rather, genuine peace is based on meeting the needs of individuals and societies for physical and spiritual well-being, which supplies meaning and freedom. All individuals and societies can grow and develop more fully. Most of the energies of the United Nations are devoted to problem solving, international cooperation, and promoting respect for human rights. Hence the work of the World Health Organization (WHO); Food and Agriculture Organization (FAO); UN Educational, Scientific, and Cultural Organization (UNESCO); United Nations Children's Fund (UNICEF); and a host of other United Nations-sponsored agencies.

All of these are at work in the Middle East. But the most widespread United Nations humanitarian activity in this region is the United Nations Relief and Works Agency for Palestine Refugees in the Near East (UNRWA). UNRWA was established as a temporary agency in 1950. Its mandate, renewed periodically by the UN General Assembly, is to provide services to Palestinian refugees who have "lost both their homes and their means of livelihood."

In 1950 this meant services to about 600,000 people at a

cost of $35 million. Today, because the refugee problem has not been solved and the population has enlarged, it means serving 850,000 out of a total 1,800,000 refugees with a 1979 budget estimate of $151.8 million. Over 600,000 refugees continue to live in UNRWA camps located in Jordan, Lebanon, Syria, and the Israeli-occupied West Bank and Gaza Strip.

During the first years of UNRWA most programs were devoted to basic survival needs—food, clothing, housing, and medicine. Today such relief services represent less than one fourth of the budget and less than 10 percent of the personnel. Education and training services are now the largest UNRWA activity using 55 percent of the budget and 65 percent of the total employees (10,700)—mostly teachers. The third area of major activity continues to be health related. In education particularly, UNRWA has been creative in developing model schools and supplying university scholarships to talented students.

It is hard to imagine what the Middle East would have been like the past thirty years without this gigantic educational and welfare program. UNRWA has provided the critical needs for nearly half of the Palestinian people. More significant than this has been its role in providing meaning and hope in a situation thought to be temporary but now appearing to be permanent. While frustration has given rise to a variety of political expressions, some violent, it is likely that the level of violence would have been much greater were it not for UNRWA.

Since 1977 UNRWA has faced a major budgetary crises. Its costs have soared because of worldwide inflation without a corresponding increase in contributions. The UNRWA budget is largely provided by sixteen governments and the European Economic Community. Retiring Commissioner General Thomas W. McElhiney, a former United States diplomat, reported at the end of 1978 that resources are no longer "adequate to maintain services." The flour ration has been reduced by 50 percent from 10 kilograms per recipient a month to five kilograms per month during the past year. Wages for employees have not been increased as fast as the inflation rate, creating considerable backlash as well as hardship. Some schools have to be closed. One reason for the early retirement of McElhiney has been the frustrations caused by continuing needs and declining resources. The United States and Canada have been major contributors to UNRWA through the years. Canada's $4 million and the United State's $50 million make up a substantial portion of the total UNRWA budget. The United States contribution of $750 million since 1950 is about half of the total budget during this entire period, but even so this represents only about $50 per refugee served per year. Nevertheless, it represents one of the finest overseas investments and deserves continuation and expansion.

Just as critical as refugee services has been the United Nations role in working for peace in this violence-prone region. To be sure, the interminable debates and frequent conferences have not led to a peaceful environment. The presence of United Nations military forces has not prevented the outbreak of hostilities. Nevertheless, it seems obvious that without a neutral go-between for the exchange of information as well as prisoners of war or the availability of interposing forces and observers that there would be even more conflict.

The core peacekeeping force is composed of 300 military observers from a dozen countries, which make up UNTSO, created to supervise the cease-fire and truce of 1948-49. These professionals have staffed observation posts along the frontiers of Israel and have served as senior advisers to the peacekeeping forces established since that time.

The second such force, UNEF, was established first in 1956 and stationed on Egyptian territory to patrol the armistice line and frontier. This force was withdrawn at the request of Egypt before the 1967 six-day war. UNEF-II was reconstituted in October 1973 to observe the cease-fire in the Sinai, where it remains. The 4,000-member force from seven countries has played an expanded role after the disengagement agreements of 1974-75. With the new agreements leading to Israel's withdrawal from the Sinai, it was assumed that UNEF would continue its role as truce observer with special responsibilities in the buffer zones between Egyptian and Israeli armies. Since the USSR opposed the bilateral Egypt-Israel peace treaty in March 1979, they have vetoed the extension of the UNEF so this peace-keeping force is being phased out.

UNDOF is similar to UNEF in purpose and function but located on the Golan Heights. Here the task is to maintain the truce between Israel and Syria. Some 1,200 persons from four countries are posted in and about the demilitarized zone.

The largest and most recent peacekeeping operation is presently located in Lebanon. UNIFIL was established by the UN Security Council in March 1978 "to (1) confirm the withdrawal of Israeli forces, (2) restore international peace and security, and (3) assist the Lebanese government in insuring the return of its effective authority in the southern part of the country." Presently over 6,000 troops from seven countries are based in the region south of the Litani River.

It has been a difficult task for UNIFIL to move into this political vacuum alongside the two intruders—the Israeli army and the Palestinian commandos. The Lebanese government is only now trying to reestablish its presence both as a police force and a welfare agency. Israel has withdrawn slowly, and in the last stage turned over authority to a former Lebanese army commander, Major Haddad, who has been declared a traitor by the Lebanese government.

UNIFIL has not yet been able to gain control over the ten kilometer strip along the Israel border. UNIFIL has been successful in providing sufficient normalcy so that most of the 100,000 refugees created by the Israeli invasion in March 1978 have returned to their homes. But there have been thirty deaths to soldiers from France, Fiji, Nigeria, Norway, Senegal, and Ireland, mostly from mines left behind by the withdrawing Israelis. UNIFIL finds itself in almost daily conflict with one or more of the military groups operating close by—Palestinian commandos, Major Haddad's Christian militia, or the Israeli army.

It has frequently been said that if there were no United Nations some similar body would need to be established to perform its many functions. No one would dispute this in the Middle East. The United Nations General Assembly and Security Council have provided a forum for debate and decision-making. The special conferences and actions are recognized by most of those involved as the basis for the resolution of the several conflicts, beginning with the 1947 action dividing Palestine continuing to Resolution 242 calling for Israeli withdrawal from the occupied territories. UNRWA for 29 years has been a quasi-governmental agency in meeting many of the physical, social, and cultural needs of the Palestinian refugees. The various peacekeeping forces haven't prevented all wars, but they have supplied an institutional base which has made possible some stability when Arabs and Israelis were unable to deal with each other.

The London-based Institute for Strategic Studies says

these experiences suggest an even greater role for United Nations peacekeeping in the region. In their *Strategic Survey 1978* they say UNIFIL units have been a model in developing a more aggressive peacekeeping role by "separating the conflicting armed elements and thus ensure peace in these areas and the protection of the local population." As such the ISS says this should "encourage Israel to consider the use of UN forces as a significant part of a Middle East settlement." The ISS particularly complimented the Ghanaian UNIFIL Commander General Emmanual Erskine for his creative leadership.

The United Nations has endured considerable criticism, some justified, for its weakness and failure, including its varied roles in the Middle East. Few people add that the United Nations is only as powerful as member states allow it to be. But it has also demonstrated that a patient, persistent commitment to negotiation and compromise is better than violence and death. In the Middle East the United Nations is a welcome insignia of peace and hope.

CHAPTER 12

FIVE PILLARS OF THE NEW MIDDLE EAST

The stay of my family and myself in Jerusalem was a most exciting ten months. We arrived just when plans for the Camp David peace colloquy were announced. We experienced the aftermath of the Israeli invasion of South Lebanon, March to June 1978. We watched the faltering follow-up to Camp David which climaxed in the peace treaty of March 1979. We eagerly followed the fall of the Shah in Iran and the predictions that Islamic forces would also threaten governments in Egypt and Syria. These and many other events made this year "the year of the Middle East" in the larger panorama of world history.

Now I'd like to summarize what appears to me to be five pillars—to use a good Middle Eastern term—or historic currents which seem to me are creating a new ecology for this region. These five are: (1) the rapid amassing of wealth, (2) the new moment of vitality in Islam, (3) the militarism and the totalitarian temptation, (4) the denouement of the thirty years' war between Arabs and Israelis, and (5) the ubiquitous American empire.

Monetary Reserves, Middle East Oil-Exporting Countries*

(In millions of dollars)

Country	1969	1970	1971	1972	1973	1974	1975	1976
Algeria	$410	$ 339	$ 507	$ 493	$1,143	$1,689	$1,353	$1,987
Egypt	145	167	161	149	391	342	294	339
Iran	310	208	621	960	1,237	8,383	8,897	8,833
Iraq	476	462	600	782	1,553	3,273	2,727	4,601
Kuwait	182	203	288	363	501	1,397	1,655	1,929
Libya	918	1,590	2,665	2,925	2,127	3,616	2,195	3,206
Saudi Arabia	607	662	1,444	2,500	3,877	14,285	23,319	27,025
Syria	59	55	88	135	481	835	735	361

*A country's international reserves consist of its reserves in gold, SDRs (special drawing rights which are unconditional international reserve assets created by the International Monetary Fund), its reserve position in the Fund (unconditional assets that arise from a country's gold subscription to the Fund and from the Fund's use of a member's currency to finance the drawings of others) and its foreign exchange (holdings by monetary authorities—such as central banks, currency boards, exchange stabilization funds and Treasuries—of claims on foreigners in the form of bank deposits, Treasury bills, government securities and other claims usable in the event of a balance of payments deficit).

SOURCE: Data from the International Monetary Fund's International Financial Statistics, June 1975, August 1977.

Because I begin with an economic factor, I do not want to appear as an economic determinist. Rather, the objective reality of Middle East wealth is simply the most obvious and most tangible current. Anyone who has traveled in the area from Libya to Iran can only be impressed by the enormous amount of building—houses, hotels, roads, and commercial centers. While great gaps in wealth continue, it is also true that in every Mideast state except Egypt and Lebanon the new wealth of the area is being applied to public services guaranteeing higher standards of health and education. All this is unfolding in a region conspicuous for poverty, malnutrition, and disease less than two decades ago.

Several statistical summaries may help us visualize this dramatic increase in wealth. First consider the chart on page 97, documenting the increase in monetary reserves.

For comparative purposes and to fill in missing countries here are several additional 1976 statistics, the most recent I have available: Jordan $491 m; Lebanon $1,677 m; Israel $1,373 m; Canada $5,843 m; United States $18,320 m.

Another set of important statistics are those at the top of the next page from the *World Development Report 1978* produced by the World Bank:

Oil has, of course, not only been fueling the world but propelling this enormous surge of monetary reserves. Mahmoud Fouad in the *Middle East Journal* (Summer 1978) says that the Middle East now provides 25 percent of the funds for World Bank and that the region "is potentially more than self-sufficient in capital . . . The deficits of Egypt, Syria, and Jordan would only absorb a small fraction of the rich Arab countries' combined surplus." In this regard the generosity of these states is striking. The OPEC states (mostly Arab plus Iran) disburse over five billion dollars of official development assistance, not including military

World Development Report 1978 Produced by the World Bank

Country	Population (1976)	GNP per capita	Annual Growth % 1970-76
Yemen Arab Rep.	6.0m	$ 250	
Yemen PDR	1.7m	280	6.3%
Egypt	38.1m	280	1.9
Jordan	2.8m	610	1.6
Syria	7.7m	780	2.2
Lebanon	3.2m	1,090	3.1
Iraq	11.5m	1,390	3.6
Iran	34.3m	1,930	8.2
Israel	3.6m	3,920	4.3
Saudi Arabia	8.6m	4,480	7.0
Libya	2.5m	6,310	10.2
Kuwait	1.1m	15,480	-3.0

grants, annually (up from $1.3 billion in 1974). This amounts to over 2.5 percent of their GNP annually compared to the one-third of one percent given by developed nations! To be sure, self-interest motivates much of this giving and most of it goes to fellow Arab or Islamic states. Nevertheless, this stands as a serious challenge for the richer, better established and, as they say in the Middle East, "Christian" countries.

Another interesting source of wealth for the peoples of the Middle East are the remittances coming from workers and/ or family members overseas. Reliable figures for this are difficult to find. Some estimates place the amount at a billion dollars per year for Jordan and Egypt alone. In the West Bank hundreds of fine houses have been built from overseas earnings. Israel is a special case with its annual grants from Jews around the world.

Beyond the visible evidences of this new wealth is the

enormous surge of confidence it has given cultures and peoples that not long ago believed that their power and glory was all in the past. But increases of this proportion also mean problems of absorption and assimilation. Most Middle East states have adopted a conservative approach, especially for releasing funds into the private sector. Some have deliberately slowed down their exports to prolong the impact. This can also be seen as a deliberate attempt to maintain a stable social order. Iran, no matter whom we blame, found this impossible. The social structure creaked with inequality, waste, corruption, and exacerbated feelings of frustration and alienation. We know the rest of the story. It is important to observe how Saudi Arabia in particular has been using an Islamic code of morality to prevent excesses of extravagance. Sadat's decision to replace Mercedes with Fiats in the government auto fleet, scorned by many, is an intelligent and concrete attempt to symbolize frugality and control a potential reaction to conspicuous consumption among his people.

The second pillar is the revival of interest in Islam. The obvious connection with the first pillar is the use of wealth to extend the faith as well as to undergird the self-image mentioned above.

Two kinds of evidence suggest this new surge of vitality. First are the visible expressions: new mosques; more women adopting distinctive dress styles (rumor says they are being paid by Libya or Saudi Arabia); abundant religious literature, much of it attractively produced in a variety of languages; more frequent pictorial and oral references to public piety by public officials. Some evidence indicates that Islam is gaining new adherents in Africa and Central Asia, but this may be somewhat exaggerated by the fears of Christian missionaries.

The second evidence of a revitalization of Islam is the pressure for political support and expression of Islamic faith and life. This can range from the call for more religious instruction in schools, such as the "Basic Obligatory Studies in Islam" required in each year of undergraduate study in Saudi Arabia, to the demand that Islamic law—*Shari'a*—become the basis of public law. This pressure is found in every Middle Eastern country. In Egypt, Syria, Jordan, Saudi Arabia, and Iraq the sheikhs are paid by the state. Often their sermons require prior censorship, so that the government maintains an effective control. In Iran, because of a long-standing conflict between the Shi'ites and the Palhavi dynasty, religion became the vehicle for political opposition and perhaps revolution.

It is doubtful that the Iranian experience portends future revolutions. Most political leaders such as Sadat and Hussein have harnessed the religious forces for their own purposes. Yet additional surprises are possible. Egypt could become an explosive situation. The Muslim Brotherhood has an enormous following in the universities. Mohammed Sid-Ahmed, an Egyptian journalist says, "The day people become aware that peace is not synonmous with prosperity, the stage could be set for the advocates of Islamic resurgence to attempt a repeat performance of Iran's revolution."

I think the why of this revival is as important as the phenomena themselves. We have already mentioned two important factors—the political use of religious enthusiasm for political as well as religious purposes, and the sense of divine blessing that accompanied the new wealth amassing to Islamic people. Closely connected to these is the opposite at work in certain places—the need for moorings in a time of rapid social change. A civilization suffering from insult and conflict will often turn to the tried and familiar. Just as religion became the vehicle for political expression in Iran, so it can be an important vehicle in maintaining identity and expanding the influence of a civilization. A rejuvenated Islam is a way to cope with the impact of the West, above all with the presence of what is perceived to be an unacceptable foreign body in its midst—the Jewish state of Israel.

Some question the staying power of Islam, but I would suggest that the real issue is the potency of the revival. This depends first on whether Islam in fact can handle the cosmic questions of modernity. The most extreme Muslim sect in Egypt, "The Repentants" who murdered a minister of re- ligious trusts, several years ago were all well-educated persons protesting the "spiritual vacuum" in Egypt. The anti-Western spirit of much recent Islamic writing has focused on the decadence and immorality of the West, another way of attacking the spiritual vacuum.

The staying power of the revival depends on yet another factor, namely finding roots within Islamic thought and experience that authentically meet the needs of modern Is- lamic people. The political dimensions of this new revival in Iran, Pakistan, Egypt, Libya, and to a degree Lebanon represents an essential ingredient (some would say it is the essence) of the Islamic achievement. But if religion is to be expressed politically and vice versa, the issues are also what kind of religious-political order will result and where is the focus—locally, regionally, or Islamdom in general?

The third current or pillar of this new environment is the most recent phase in the search for authentic and legitimate political structures. The Shah, as one Gulf States minister said, "insulted Islam and tyrannized his people." He was overthrown. Khomeini is now searching for ways to imple- ment an Islamic Republic. The most recent information sug- gests this will be guaranteed by a national religious body which can review, ratify, or reject the actions of the government, a kind of national caliph.

This search for an appropriate Islamic politics has been going on at least since the fall of the Ottoman Empire and the abolition of the caliphate in 1924. Two relatively recent developments make the new political orders different. One is the adoption of modern technological means of governing. Most of us in the West are so accustomed to the telephone, electronic media, and bureaucratic organization that we forget how new they are in the Middle East. (The collapse of the telephone system in Beirut and Cairo is a good reminder that technological development is not inevitable.)

More critical for this analysis is the use of modernity to enforce a near totalitarian control. The Middle East has long been accustomed to authoritarian regimes. But technology, propaganda, and religio-nationalistic ideologies are now intertwined in ways that threaten personal freedom and minority allegiances more than ever. The dividing line between popular opinion and enforced opinion is delicate and often hard to locate. We don't have pogroms at this moment comparable to the Russian and Nazi attack on minorities. Yet the potential in the Middle East is very real. One Israeli analyist says, "Jewish Israel is in a real sense a totalitarian society . . . which rests not on coercion and institutional violence but on national consensus regarding Jewish and Zionist values." This same person talks of the "impressive and terrifying revival of fundamentalist Islamic integralism" in Iran. Others have pointed out the parallels between the right-wing political chauvinism of a Rabbi Kahene in Israel and the Ayatollah Khomeini in Iran. While it would be wrong to load on Israel all the responsibility for the growing strength of the conservative wing in Islam, it is nevertheless clear that the presence, and sometimes threat, of Israel has weakened the influence of "Arab liberalism" so strong before 1950.

This "integralism," real and potential, in these and other Middle East states is especially critical for any minority group. It is certainly one reason for the fear one observes among the Copts in Egypt. This development also puts into perspective the pain many feel in the collapse of Lebanon, one attempt (albeit imperfect) to develop a political structure on other than a totalitarian basis. And certainly the PLO is feared not only because of its terrorism, which even Israeli leaders see as ineffectual, but rather for the commitment of most PLO groups to a "secular, democratic state," a revolutionary portent for every state based on a political-religious ideology.

The threat of totalitarianism has been made more real by the frequent wars, powerful military establishments, and escalating accumulations of weaponry.

The militarism of the region is, on the one hand, so obvious that it requires no elaboration. On the other hand, this is a relatively new factor. Until 1972, if we were graphing expenditures, military spending was increasing at approximately the rate of inflation, well below three billion dollars per year. Since then, the line on the graph goes almost straight up—now close to thirty billion dollars per year! The Middle East outside of the United States and the USSR is the most heavily armed region in the world. Over 20 percent of the combined GNP is spent on defense compared to Europe's 7 percent. Seven of the ten leading arms importers in the developing world are located here.

The United States alone increased its military transfers to the Middle East from $4.6 billion in 1970-72 to $10.6 billion during 1973-75. During fiscal 1980 the United States is giving, loaning, or selling military goods worth over $3 billion to the region apart from the special grants totaling $5 billion tied to Egypt-Israel peace agreement. England, France, and Russia are also major arms suppliers to the region.

More critical is the way large military establishments erode any semblance of the democratic process, tend to supply political leadership, undergird the ruling parties, and displace civilian needs in the national budgets. The following table from Howard H. Frederick, *The Arms Trade and the Middle East* (Philadelphia, 1977), though several years old, dramatically displays the objective reality.

No matter what the specific issue at stake, this kind of militarism is a continual threat to peace and makes the fourth pillar in the new environment, the nearing climax in the thirty years' war between the Arab states and Israel, so

The Middle East Military Balance Sheet, 1976

(Sources: USACDA and the International Institute for Strategic Studies, London)

KEY: 1. Total armed forces; 2. Total aircraft; 3. Total navalcraft; 4. Total tanks; 5. 1974 military expenditure; 6. Military expenditure as a percentage of GNP; 7. Military expenditure per capita

	Egypt	Syria	Iraq	Jordan	TOTAL Arab	Israel
1.	410,000	130,000	110,000	70,000	720,000	160,000
2.	718	471	378	66	1,633	677
3.	30	6	8	–	44	19
4.	2,000	2,100	1,300	440	5,840	2,700
5.	$2.1 bill.	$.489 bill.	$1.04 bill.	$.137 bill.	$3.776 bill.	$3.84 bill
6.	19.8%	16.5%	13.1%	12.9%	15.6%	37.3%
7.	$53	$62	$88	$48	$63	$1030

ominous. In March 1979 the *Guardian* reporter David Hirst suggested that the next sixty days were the most critical in terms of a regional war since Israel involved Lebanon in March 1978. An American Jewish reporter more recently predicted that Israel will not withdraw from the territories without another war and that this will be sooner rather than later. Other journalists suggested that the peace treaty might not last a year since the treaty didn't really deal with the vital issue—the Palestinians. Israeli General Mattityahu Peled, an active leader of the peace forces, called the March 1978 peace treaty "worthless" and predicted that in six months "everything will fall apart."

All the above, plus the massive nonviolent shutdown of the West Bank on March 26 to mark the "humiliation" of the ignored Palestinians, and the shedding of blood by Israeli troops in Birzeit and Halhul, suggest that a new crisis can explode at any moment.

No one in the Middle East seems optimistic that this crisis can be resolved peaceably. The quarrel over autonomy appears to be so fundamental, the unity of the Palestinians so visible, and the stance of the Israeli government so rigid that the pessimists might be right. Such a judgment must be taken seriously in light of potential rekindling of civil war in Lebanon or the expansion of the conflict in Yemen.

I hope the pessimists are mistaken this time. After all, as recently as October 1978 the Shah was considered invincible. One can never be too confident in scrutinizing current affairs. Some new initiative such as a proposal for a demilitarized independent West Bank and Gaza on the part of the PLO could set in motion irresistible forces. At the same time the settlement policies of the Begin government could generate such countervailing forces that a new government may indeed need to opt for total withdrawal now considered unthinkable. Simha Flapan, editor of the pro peace *New Outlook*, and General Peled have both suggested that "Israel is facing its moment of truth. . . . The erosion of the official anti-Palestinian policy has visibly set in among almost all political parties . . . but the policy still exerts a powerful grip on the public opinion." All of this must be seen against the backdrop of the revived power of Israeli Arabs who threaten a major revision in the borders of Israel.

Finally there is the critical role of the United States in the Middle East which I call the fifth pillar. On my first trip to the region in June 1965 the American presence in Egypt was very weak while Lebanon was the biggest recipient of United States aid. Now things have dramatically changed. The United States has little influence in Lebanon and is conspicuously present in Egypt. In 1965 the United States was friendly to Israel but third to France and England in supplying arms. The war of 1967 and especially the conflict in 1973 changed this sharply.

The American presence throughout the region is conspicuous not only in the amount of money given, loaned, and invested, but also in numbers of Americans living here. These range from dozens in Lebanon, Syria, and Yemen to hundreds in Jordan and the Gulf, and thousands in Egypt, Saudi Arabia, and Israel. The total business investment, apart from government aid, in the latter three states, ranks in the billions of dollars. While the numbers representing American churches are down from the great age of missions, the great age of philanthrophy is here with numerous agencies and causes represented. Among the most fascinating groups of people in the Middle East are the voluntary agency people who are the sons and daughters of the former missionaries or who were partially educated at the great monuments to the mission achievement—the American University of Cairo (AUC) and the American University of Beirut (AUB). Finally, we must include the annual invasion of almost one million American tourists.

As in every imperial relationship, large quantities of

people and money circulate from the colonies to the host country. These include two million Arab Americans and as many Israeli citizens in New York City as in Tel Aviv. The emigration continues, along with tens of thousands of students studying in American institutions. The Saudis have invested tens of billions of dollars in United States Treasury bonds alone. The two oil crises (1973-74 and 1978-79) are reminders of how dependent the American economy has become on fuel from the Middle East. Today the United States imports 30 percent of its oil from the Middle East and this is destined to increase to 40 percent before leveling off.

The real issue is whether the American involvement is a force for peace and stability in the region. In an age of global economic entanglements there is a certain inevitability to this presence, if not this empire. But the questions of style (conspicuous or inconspicuous, forthright or low key) and alignments in terms of local conflicts have enormous influence on its character. And if American conflicts are taken into the area or area conflicts are made part of American ones this can only increase the martial climate rather than contribute to peace.

I remain highly skeptical of all kinds of empires. When I heard an American voluntary agency director exclaim the day after the peace treaty was signed that American Ambassador Lewis in Tel Aviv sounded like ambassadors he knew so well in Saigon eight years before in their similar attitudes toward these agencies, I squirmed. Whatever the American President thinks and no matter his sense of mission, peace and stability in the Middle East are primarily the tasks of the people there. It is an American problem to the extent the United States chooses to make it one. And seeing the total picture of armaments, military advisers, and alliances to several states suggests that America is more a destabilizer than a stabilizer. One thing Washington and the president certainly need to learn and relearn is that there are limits to what any nation can do, even the United States.

This short survey is at many points incomplete. Others would choose different pillars or add additional ones. Perhaps if I had spent this year in another Middle Eastern setting I would have felt more deeply regarding the Zbigniew Brzezinski's "arc of crisis" or what the magazine *Events* calls the "ring of iron." While I do not doubt Russian machinations, their very nearness and considerable past involvements mean greater suspicion and hostility to their presence than to the other superpower.

The point is that a new ecology has emerged in the Middle East. Compare the situation today with that in 1950 soon after the establishment of Israel and the new independence of the other states when the region was impoverished. At that time Islam was dazed by nationalist movements within and the shattering presence of Israel; no state was strong militarily and, though there were strong rulers, most were of a traditional personalist kind; modernization had not progressed far enough to enable a genuinely totalitarian social order; the Arab states and Israel had no idea that they would or could wage a war for more than thirty years; the American presence in all the Mideast states, except perhaps Saudi Arabia, was dwarfed by England and France, and even the Soviet Union had almost as much influence in Israel. While recognizing the fact of newness I would emphasize that these five representative historic currents will not soon be superseded.

Yet I must hasten to add that numerous observers say that Middle East politics has not been so fluid since the early 1950s as today. One of Egypt's most perceptive commentators Mohammed Sid-Ahmed said he wouldn't want to predict the outcome. That's why I liked the BBC report from Jerusalem on March 12 quoting several White House staff members. "The situation is fluid. . . . We are either coming or going."

CHAPTER 13

TRYING TO THINK ETHICALLY IN JERUSALEM

If there is anyplace one ought to think ethically, it is in Jerusalem. Here, if anywhere, considerations of right and wrong should be apparent and paramount. Peace and justice ought to be the obvious concern in the city of *Shalom/Salaam*, peace. Yet the obvious is far from a reality. Already in ancient times the psalmist admonished worshipers to "pray for the peace of Jerusalem." The Old Testament prophets lamented the truthlessness, injustice, and idolatry of Jerusalem while longing for the perfection of the heavenly Jerusalem. The religiosity of modern Jerusalem is conspicuous. The moral sensitivity of modern Jerusalem is less apparent.

Yet to be a responsible Jerusalemite, even if for a short time, one ought to search for what might make this city truly a city of peace today. To avoid working for the things that make for peace is to deny not only the meaning of Jerusalem but to contribute to the violence and hostility that make the city unholy. Like all the other essays in this volume, this topic deserves book-length treatment. Here we can only suggest how one might think ethically. My own point of view about ethics has been well stated by the German Protestant martyr of World War II, Dietrich Bonhoeffer:

> Ethics as formation means the bold endeavour to speak about the way in which the form of Jesus Christ takes form in our world, in a manner which is neither abstract nor casuistic, neither programmatic nor purely speculative. ... Ethics as formulation is possible only upon the foundation of the form of Jesus Christ which is present in His church. The church is the place where Jesus Christ's taking form is proclaimed and accomplished. (*Ethics*, 1965, p. 88).

Thinking ethically first of all means taking concerns for right and wrong and values like peace and justice seriously. Because of the complexity of the modern world and the difficulty of sorting out how to make one's values felt, many of us in Jerusalem and most other cities in the world try to avoid thinking ethically. We usually prefer to let those in government make the hard decisions. We might think that whatever is going on must be correct, or that it is no use to think ethically since evil prevails and can be overcome only in the conversion of individuals. In Jerusalem it is easy to politicize ethics and say that might makes right or to nationalize one's point of view identifying with Israelis by saying Israel is always right or with the Palestinians by claiming the opposite.

Yet the great religious traditions of Jerusalem—Judaism, Christianity, and Islam—all emphasize moral and ethical thinking. The first and great commandment of each begins with the assertion that "the Lord our God is one Lord and you shall love the Lord your God with all your heart and with all your soul and with all your might" and "you shall love your neighbor as yourself." Each of the Jerusalem religions have failed to fulfill this high standard.

This commandment suggests three criteria for thinking ethically. The first is the need for a vision of peaceful, just, and purposeful human relationships. The Hebrew word for peace is *shalom,* translated into Arabic as *salaam* and into English as peace. When the term peace is used in English versions of the Old Testament, it is almost always a translation of shalom which refers to a community of harmony and security where each individual finds joy and fulfillment in the well-being of every other. Shalom looks backward to the ideal of the Garden of Eden and forward to final healing of all creation in a new heaven and new earth. The people of God are those who covenant together to live by God's grace as a people of peace. Ethically, thinking begins with this vision.

The second insight into ethical thinking derived from the great commandment is a set of values to be applied in concrete human experiences. The vision is to be lived. Values such as peace, truth, love, and justice become the basis for deciding as well as thinking. It is obvious that there is much violence, untruth, hatred, and injustice in human affairs. But it is precisely because good and evil both find expression in the world that ethical thinking requires choices. These choices are never simple or easy. Sometimes the choice has to do with a specific act such as a terrorist attack, but more likely ethical analysis has to do with the system of evil which involves ideas of sovereignty and security or the distortions of prejudice and ideology. These values should guide thinking about means as well as ends. As the great Jewish philosopher Martin Buber observed nearly fifty years ago, "If the goal to be reached is like the goal which was set, then the nature of the way must be like the goal. A wrong way, i.e., a way in contradiction to the goal, must lead to a wrong goal."

Third, the great commandment suggests that people who put their ultimate commitments in love of God and love of the neighbor have to work as hard at deciding what is ethically correct as nations do to prove that their course of action is best. The New Testament says one of the gifts of the Holy Spirit to the believer is the ability to test the spirits, to discern the will of God, to understand the signs of the times. So ethical thinking means probing the Scriptures, listening to the Holy Spirit, studying the issue and situation, and then after discussion with other seekers distinguishing and sorting out, deciding and acting.

On most great issues, certainly issues in the Middle East, no one side or party is all right or all wrong. It is equally true that religious and national loyalties distort ethical thinking more than any other forces. (One of my Jerusalem friends calls Jerusalem the world capital of idolatry for this very reason.) The task of discerning does not mean that choices are between absolutes but rather that one action, one policy is more correct or more incorrect than another. Whatever the decision there is no room for self-righteousness since as the Apostle Paul says, "All have sinned and fall short of the glory of God." The Protestant ethicist John C. Bennett summarizes this need for study and discernment in ethical thinking about public affairs with his dictum that "Christian faith and ethics offer ultimate perspectives, broad criteria, motives, inspirations, sensibilities, warnings, moral limits rather than directives for policies and decisions."

There should be no need to list the issues that require ethical thinking in Jerusalem. There are the obvious abuses of people which climax in murder and deportation, the expropriation of land, the violation of human rights, hatred and prejudice, and the misuse of resources. Both Arabs and Jews have been the victims of systematic attacks on their peoplehood, resulting in massive suffering from war and other forms of criminality. When Palestinian commandos attack innocent tourists and Israeli soldiers strike civilian targets the concerned and thoughtful observer will look not only at what happened but the general situation that made such action possible.

It is not our purpose here to analyze either the general situation or specific actions. Rather, anyone who thinks about the peace of Jerusalem ought to realize that there is something wrong that this city, perhaps more than any other single factor, has been the cause and center of violence in the Middle East for the past fifty years. Its very name suggests that there is another way. Anyone who thinks about Jerusalem, at least Western Christians, will need to recognize their own involvement in this seemingly perpetual evil. Western Christians have been the anti-Semites whose prejudice against Jews and Arabs has been a primary cause of the present-day struggle. Americans and Canadians have helped to supply armaments which are now used for destructive purposes by both sides. Ethical thinking begins with a recognition of involvement, a sense of modesty, and the need for forgiveness.

Today, I believe, Christians who are serious about their thinking ethically (can they be otherwise?) must find ways of bringing healing and compassion to Jerusalem and the surrounding region as never before. Now it is necessary to highlight the evil and shortsightedness of violent solutions to political problems. Now is the time to proclaim the integrity of individuals and peoples. Now is the time to speak the truth to ourselves, and those immediately involved, about freedom and security—the most distorted terms used in the Middle East today. Now is the time for the ethically concerned to work to change attitudes and develop a strategy for active involved peacemaking. This will begin with our own attitudes, our churches, our nation, and then participation in programs to reduce the threat of violence and increase the stake of individuals, groups, and nations in the peaceful resolution of conflicts.

Adam Curle, the British Quaker who has thought much and worked hard to find peaceful means of conflict resolution, focuses the task of ethical thinking anywhere but especially in Jerusalem with these wise words.

Rather than believe that one of the participants is the aggressor and the other the victim he [the peacemaker] should discipline himself to concentrate his sympathies on all those who are suffering as a result of the conflict: the soldiers and civilians who have been killed, wounded or deprived; the statesmen faced by agonizing choices; the children who have lost their fathers; all the people whose lives are being made harder and less happy; the millions whose lives are being twisted by propaganda. From this standpoint it is irrelevant to think who is right and who is wrong: it is war itself that is wrong as a means of settling human disputes. (*Making Peace*, 1971, p. 240).

A Checklist of Topics to Consider in the Search for Peace Between Israel and the Palestinians

As the essays in this book indicate, the conflict between Israelis and Palestinians is very complex. There are several levels and a long history that intersects and overlaps. Here is a listing of the many topics and subtopics that must go into any comprehensive analysis.

I. The historic realities: what actually happened and perceptions of what happened.
    A. Conflicting claims and conflicts in Palestine since the second millennium BC.
    B. Comparative economic and technological development of the several states and localities.
    C. The nineteenth-century disintegration of the Ottoman Empire and European imperial rivalries.
    D. The role and impact of the imperial forces which have ruled Palestine.
    E. The Jewish experience in Palestine, the Middle East, and Europe.
    F. The Arab experience and the rise of Arab nationalism.
    G. The Arab Israeli Wars: 1948, 1956, 1967, 1973 with intermittent conflicts, terrorism, and retaliation.

II. The politics and diplomacy of the established states and nationalist movements.
   A. The character, structure, and style of the states involved and the nationalist movements.
   B. The impact of war; the role of the military and guerrilla organizations in each state.
   C. The major Palestinian resistance organizations and their role in the Palestine Liberation Organization.
   D. The significance of individual leaders and theoreticians in states and movements at different moments.
   E. External relationships of states and organizations to major world powers and with other states in the region.
   F. The nature of the Israeli military occupation.
   G. The United Nations peacekeeping forces.

III. Refugees and Minorities
   A. The treatment of linguistic, ethnic, and religious minorities throughout Middle Eastern history.
   B. Present-day refugees: definition, numbers, location, status.
   C. The nature of "homelessness" for a family-oriented, agrarian, nationalistic peoples.
   D. The creating of Palestinian refugees: partition, war, flight.
   E. Possibilities for resettlement in Israel or West Bank. Emigration to other Arab states and other continents.
   F. The welfare system provided refugees by host states and the United Nations, as well as national policies on refugees.
   G. Jewish refugees: during and after World War II from Europe; from Arab countries after 1948.

IV. The Search for Peace
   A. Pre-1948 proposals: the success/failure of the British Mandate government.
   B. The shifting interests and demands of the participants and interested parties.

    C. The shifting role and proposals of the United Nations and world powers.

    D. The overt and covert meaning of the code words: justice, rights, security. Comprehensive or step-by-step diplomacy.

    E. Historical developments and the peace process: Arab-Israeli wars, cold war, military occupations, settlements in the occupied territories, competition over resources—land, water, oil.

V. Religious Considerations

    A. The meaning of land, war and peace, religious and political freedom in Judaism, Eastern Christianity, and Islam.

    B. The historical experience of Judaism, Eastern Christianity, and Islam with each other and within the imperial dominions.

    C. The religious quality of the contemporary conflict.

    D. International religious interests and influence in Israel-Palestine and the contemporary conflict.

    E. The role of mission societies and voluntary agencies within the region and worldwide public opinion.

    F. Pacifist groups and individuals and their impact on the peace process—local, national, global.

VI. Issues requiring attention in any comprehensive peace settlement.

    A. The attitudes and rhetoric of peoples and nations involved.

    B. Freedom and security for the people—minorities and majorities—throughout the region.

    C. Allocation of resources: land, oil, water—including the Jordan River Valley and the Dead Sea.

    D. Resettlement of and/or the return of Arab refugees to the West Bank and Israel.

    E. Dismanteling of military governments in West Bank and Gaza, reduction of military forces throughout the region, elimination of guerrilla forces, renunciation of terrorist attempts and preemptive retaliation.

F. New self-governing arrangements in the presently occupied territories including police and public welfare authority.

G. Development of effective national boundaries with definitions of sovereignty legitimacy for the states involved.

H. The status of East Jerusalem.

I. A financial settlement for Arab property in pre-1967 Israel and Israeli investments in the occupied territories.

J. Freedom of movement of people and materials throughout the region as well as cooperative regional planning.

K. The support of neighboring states and the great powers in peace settlement.

L. The development of structures for the resolution of new and continuing conflicts.

Suggestions for Further Reading

A massive amount of literature is available on Israel, Palestine, and the Middle East. I have listed here twenty good titles that cover the issues dealt with in this book. Most of these books include additional bibliographical suggestions. Periodical literature is also voluminous. Some of the best ways of keeping up to date from the Middle East itself are through *The Jerusalem Post* International Edition (weekly), the *Middle East* (monthly), *New Outlook* (monthly), and the *Journal of Palestine Studies* (quarterly). The Israel Information Center, Jerusalem; the Arab Information Center, New York; Americans for Middle East Understanding, New York; and the Institute of Palestine Studies, Beirut, are additional sources of current opinion.

Abramov, S. Zalman. *Perpetual Dilemma: Jewish Religion in a Jewish State*. Rutherford, N.J.: Fairleigh Dickinson University Press, 1976.

American Friends Service Committee. *Search for Peace in the Middle East*. New York: A. S. Barnes, 1976.

Avnery, Uri. *Israel Without Zionists*. New York: Macmillan, 1971.

Betts, Robert B. *Christians in the Arab East*. Atlanta: John Knox, 1978.

Buber, Martin. *Israel and the World*. New York: Schocken Books, 1978.

Chomsky, Noam. *Peace in the Middle East?* New York: Random House, 1975.

Cragg, Kenneth. *The Call of the Minaret*. New York: Oxford University Press, 1966.

Eban, Abba. *Autobiography*. New York: Random House, 1977.

Elon, Amos. *The Israelis: Founders and Sons*. New York: Bantam Books, 1972.

Epp, Frank. *Whose Land Is Palestine?* Grand Rapids: Eerdmans, 1970.

Hertzberg, Arthur (ed.). *The Zionist Idea*. New York: Atheneum, 1977.

Hirst, David. *The Gun and the Olive Branch: The Roots of Violence in the Middle East*. London: Faber and Faber, 1977.

Khadduri, Majid. *Political Trends in the Arab World*. Baltimore: John Hopkins University Press, 1970.

Laqueur, Walter. *The Israel-Arab Reader*. New York: Bantam Books, 1971.

Lewis, Bernard. *The Arabs in History*. New York: Harper & Row, 1966.

Mansfield, Peter. *The Arabs*. New York: Penguin Books, 1978.

Quandt, William, *et al*. *The Politics of Palestine Nationalism*. Berkeley: University of California Press, 1973.

Safran, Nadav. *Israel: The Embattled Ally*. Cambridge, Mass.: Harvard University Press, 1978.

Said, Edward. *Orientalism*. New York: Pantheon Books, 1978.

Sid-Ahmed, Mohammed. *When the Guns Fall Silent*. New York: St. Martins, 1976.

John A. Lapp is Dean of the College and Professor of History at Goshen College, Goshen, Indiana. He holds the PhD degree from University of Pennsylvania, an MA from Case-Western Reserve University, and the BA from Eastern Mennonite College. In 1965, Lapp was a Fulbright Fellow at the Summer Institute in Indian Civilization in New Delhi.

Lapp became interested in the Middle East while Executive Secretary of the Mennonite Central Committee (MCC) Peace Section, Akron, Pennsylvania, between 1969 and 1972. He traveled in the Middle East for Mennonite Central Committee in 1969 and 1974. During his sabbatical year in Jerusalem, he served as a consultant to the MCC program. While in the region he traveled in Egypt, Lebanon, Jordan, Syria, Israel, Cyprus, and Turkey.

Since 1963, Lapp has written a monthly column on current affairs for *Christian Living* magazine. He is the author of *The Mennonite Church in India, 1897-1962* (Herald Press, 1972), *A Dream for America* (Herald Press, 1976), as well as chapters in *Kingdom, Cross and Community* (Herald Press, 1976) and *Evangelicalism and Anabaptism* (Herald Press, 1979).

John A. and Alice Weber Lapp are the parents of John F., Jennifer, and Jessica.